The books in the series also provide a segue to the foundation volume that offers the most comprehensive textbook treatment available dealing with all the major issues, approaches, institutions, and actors in contemporary global governance—our edited work *International Organization and Global Governance* (2014)—a volume to which many of the authors in the series have contributed essays.

Understanding global governance—past, present, and future—is far from a finished journey. The books in this series nonetheless represent significant steps toward a better way of conceiving contemporary problems and issues as well as, hopefully, doing something to improve world order. We value the feedback from our readers and their role in helping shape the on-going development of the series.

A complete list of titles appears at the end of this book. The most recent titles in the series are:

The United Nations Centre on Transnational Corporations (2015)
by Khalil Hamdani and Lorraine Ruffing

The Challenges of Constructing Legitimacy in Peacebuilding (2015)
by Daisaku Higashi

The European Union and Environmental Governance (2015)
by Henrik Selin and Stacy D. VanDeveer

Rising Powers, Global Governance, and Global Ethics (2015)
edited by Jamie Gaskarth

Wartime Origins and the Future United Nations (2015)
edited by Dan Plesch and Thomas G. Weiss

International Judicial Institutions (2nd edition, 2015)
by Richard J. Goldstone and Adam M. Smith

The NGO Challenge for International Relations Theory (2015)
edited by William E. DeMars and Dennis Dijkzeul

Global Corporations in Global Governance

Christopher May

Routledge
Taylor & Francis Group

LONDON AND NEW YORK

First published 2015
by Routledge
2 Park Square, Milton Park, Abingdon, Oxon OX14 4RN

and by Routledge
711 Third Avenue, New York, NY 10017

Routledge is an imprint of the Taylor & Francis Group, an informa business

British Library Cataloguing in Publication Data
A catalogue record for this book is available from the British Library

Library of Congress Cataloging in Publication Data
May, Christopher N.
Global corporations in global governance / Christopher May.
    pages cm. – (Routledge global institutions series ; 99)
Includes bibliographical references and index.
    1. Corporate governance–International cooperation. 2. Global governance. 3. International business enterprises–Political aspects. I. Title.
    HD2741.M34 2015
    338.8'8–dc23
            2014037817

ISBN: 978-0-415-71603-1 (hbk)
ISBN: 978-0-415-71605-5 (pbk)
ISBN: 978-1-315-88020-4 (ebk)

Typeset in Times New Roman
by Taylor & Francis Books

MIX
Paper from
responsible sources
FSC
www.fsc.org   FSC® C013604

Printed and bound by CPI Group (UK) Ltd, Croydon, CR0 4 ›

Contents

Acknowledgments

Having worked in the private sector before I joined the academy, I have always maintained an interest in the corporate sector, prompting me some years ago to edit *Global Corporate Power* when serving as co-series editor of the IPE Yearbooks series. Although my main research has now moved from a focus on intellectual property rights to the question of the normative role of the idea of the rule of law, I have maintained this interest in the political economy of the corporate sector. This book is the result of a conversation between Rorden Wilkinson (one of the series editors) and myself, and builds on my teaching a course at Lancaster University on corporations. A previous book—*The Information Society: a skeptical view*—benefited greatly from being written in parallel to teaching an undergraduate course on the subject, and I hope that this will prove to be the case again here. The students who took that course in 2013/14 were a great aid in helping decide the level of detail and focus of coverage that would most interest readers. I would like to thank: Nathan Masih-Hanneghan who very kindly read the entire manuscript at a late stage to judge its accessibility; all the students on the course helped me clarify what needed to be said about a range of subjects, but I would also like to especially thank Chris Moore, Josh Roebuck, and Max Dieter who asked some great questions in seminars. Finally as always Hilary Jagger, my wife is a great support and as we reach our 30th wedding anniversary this year, I know it would be impossible to do what I do without having her as an oasis of good sense nearby.

Abbreviations

AGM	Annual general meeting
ATCA	US Alien Tort Claims Act
BITs	Bilateral Investment Treaties
CEO	Chief executive officer
CSI	Coalition of Service Industries
CSR	Corporate social responsibility
DSM	Dispute settlement mechanism, World Trade Organization
ECJ	European Court of Justice
EU	European Union
FDI	Foreign Direct Investment
GATS	General Agreement on Trade in Services (World Trade Organization)
GDP	Gross domestic product
IATA	International Air Transport Association
IASB	International Accounting Standards Board
ICAO	International Civil Aviation Organization
IFRS	International Financial Reporting Standards
IGO	Intergovernmental organization
MNC	Multinational corporation
NGO	Nongovernmental organization
OECD	Organisation for Economic Co-operation and Development
RDS	Royal Dutch Shell
SCM	Subsidies and Countervailing Measures agreement, World Trade Organization
TABD	Transatlantic Business Dialogue
TRIMs	Trade Related Investment Measures agreement (World Trade Organization)

x   *Abbreviations*

TRIPs	Trade Related Aspects of Intellectual Property Rights agreement (World Trade Organization)
UN	United Nations
UNCTC	United Nations Centre on Transnational Corporations
UNCTAD	United Nations Conference on Trade and Development
UNGC	United Nations Global Compact
WEF	World Economic Forum
WIPO	World Intellectual Property Organization
WTO	World Trade Organization

Introduction
What are global corporations?

- Global corporations: a (very) short history
- Terminological exactitude, the retention of national characteristics, and the size of (global) corporations
- The importance of corporate legal form(s)
- The rest of the book

In his famous *Devil's Dictionary*, Ambrose Bierce defined a "corporation" as an "ingenious device for obtaining individual profit without individual responsibility."[1] Although things are a little more complicated than that, Bierce's pithy definition conveys an essential truth that we will explore in some detail in this book. Moreover, it has become a commonplace proposition that corporations have grown in importance in the (now) global political economy over the last 100 years. On the eve of the First World War, although the corporation as an economic actor already had a long history encompassing international trading companies like the Dutch East India Company and multilateral clan or family based banking concerns such as those of the Rothschild family (and before them the Medici), in the main companies and corporations still remained mostly focused on their domestic markets and economies. Certainly they may have imported and exported goods but most corporations were at most *international*, active among a relatively small number of countries. Moving forward through the twentieth century, transport innovations, such as the standard sized shipping container,[2] and cheap long-range communication technologies including the now largely forgotten telex and fax machines, supported the development of ever more complex and more widely geographically focused corporations. We are often told, 15 years into the new millennium, that these developments have resulted in a global corporate economy; that in many (although not necessarily all) sectors corporations link economies and countries together in a global market. However, this book is not about the rise of the global corporation, although its rise plays a part in my analysis; what I explore in the following chapters is the inter-relationship between global corporations as a multi-faceted and diverse group of political actors, and the development of the institutions and practices of global governance in the period that followed the end of the Cold War.

The quarter-century since Presidents Reagan and Gorbachev negotiated the end of the Cold War, and the nearly 50-year standoff between the communist and capitalist blocs, has seen a re-conceptualization of the global political economic space. Often presented as the result of globalization, a process that sometimes seems to lack causes (other than an often reified process of technological change) and even actors, this period has seen the accelerating expansion of a global economic realm occupied by corporations, often presented by commentators as ever more detached from any national political economic control. Although not the only factor, this development has nevertheless played an important part in encouraging interest in, and engagement with the idea of global governance, in itself developed in part as the ongoing attempt by the supporters of the United Nations to bring the rule of law to international relations. As international relations have become more complex and multi-dimensional, so the political desire to find law-like methods of regulation has grown. Thus, global corporations and new institutions of global governance have both found an environment favorable to their expansion in the post-Cold War global political economy, and it is the relationship between these two expansionary dynamics that I seek to explore here. Moreover, as will become clear, global corporations are themselves important institutions in the global political economy with their own specific forms, structures, and behaviors; this is to say the institutions of global governance impact on global corporate practices *and* global corporations within their own operative realms often are effectively institutions of global governance themselves.

However, before setting out on this journey it is as well to offer some brief historical context as regards the legal form of corporations (the manner in which they can be distinguished from other collective actors) and clear up some common misunderstandings about how we might discuss this particular multi-faceted group or organizations. While recognizing that there are other forms of company or private commercial enterprise, it is almost always the case that those that are active at the global level are incorporated in a national jurisdiction (or constituted through parallel legal forms). As such, I focus on corporations and make no attempt to account for globally active companies organized differently (perhaps most obviously large multinational partnerships, or globally active private firms of which perhaps IKEA is the prime example); indeed as regards regulation and practice, there is much that is parallel between these two groups and although accepting there are differences, here I take the similarities as being more important. In the rest of this chapter I offer a brief illustrative history of the corporation as a legal entity, discuss some imprecision in the terminology often used to discuss these businesses, and explain how we might understand their size and (national) characteristics. I also look at some of the key legal elements of the corporation in advance of the more detailed later discussion of these issues. This introduction concludes with an indication of how I develop the analysis in the rest of the book.

Global corporations: a (very) short history

The origins of the corporate idea (that a group organized for a specific task or goal can be treated as a single person for legal purposes) are far from clear, but may be traced back to 2000 BC and the Assyrian Empire, although this is related more to organizational issues than any legal definition of the corporation.[3] Somewhat later, in the Roman Empire, not only settlements, towns, and other colonies (as single entities), but also commercial or business organizations of artisans organized by skill or trade, were able to formally adopt a legal personality; indeed this idea of associations based on activity (rather than on proximity or residence) was to have considerable influence in legal systems influenced by Roman law.[4] More directly the origins of the modern corporation may lie with the rise of Benedictine monastic orders, and the rules under which they were organized; the accumulation of wealth by holy orders was not dissimilar to contemporary corporate activities.[5] These religious orders were early examples of groups organized through rules and practices that transcended the individual (here, of course, incorporating the will of God); likewise groups of artisans organizing themselves into what would become professional guilds also were moving towards a self-perception of belonging to a group that had some existence beyond the involvement of its individual members.

In what we might call the middle ages, in Britain and on the European continent, (proto) incorporation mostly remained limited to organizations such as universities, ecclesiastical orders, and boroughs, all of which sought to be recognized as entities beyond the life span of any specific set of members.[6] As Colin Cooke put it: the "starting-point of the corporate administrative and commercial life of today was when the towns-folk broke the links with the old economy and jurisdiction,

and became corporations of freemen, burghers or guilds."[7] Incorporation established the separation of the organization from its members,
similar to how the state was slowly being divided from the personality
of the sovereign, and allowed an element of self-governance for the
group concerned. Thus, early guilds were effectively corporate entities,
seeking to establish rules and procedures relating to the control of
specific trades, beyond the life span of any specific set or group of
artisans. However, as new technologies and trades began to be developed outside the traditional guild structures in the late sixteenth century, the common law assumption of a form of legal personality started
more frequently to be extended to business enterprises that reached
beyond the relatively local horizons of the guilds.[8] The East India
Company, the Royal African Company, and the Hudson's Bay Company were among the first commercial (non-guild) organizations to be
incorporated by charter, and such trading companies were the first
corporate entities to reach out beyond the borders of their home
country with a strategic intent rather than merely as an opportunistic
response to specific circumstances.[9] Previous commercial activities
notwithstanding, these were the first international (or multinational)
corporations, but because management and control practices were as
yet under developed, often these entities merely formalized family and
kinship relations.[10] Likewise the renaissance banking families, such as
the Rothschild's or the Medici, also operated across Europe, but again
were organized by kin, and as such remained essentially pre-modern.
The modern corporation while prefigured by these developments, still
had not been developed in its recognizable legal form.

Indeed, the law of corporations in Britain was only finally codified
by William Blackstone in his Commentaries on the Law of England
(published in the eighteenth century), but as John P. Davis pointed out,
he "did little more than to bring together the principles scattered
through [Sir Edward] Coke's Institutes and Reports, and to present
them in a more compact and serviceable form."[11] As this suggests,
by the end of the seventeenth century these legal structures had
become standardized and incorporation was being utilized much more
widely than the previous guild arrangements. In 1702, the increasingly
important role that corporations were playing in the British economy
prompted the anonymous publication of the first book devoted to "The
Law of Corporations."[12] Both in this book and in the charters of the new
corporations, one of the key corporate undertakings was the public
goal of the better management and ordering of the trade in which the
corporation was engaged, alongside any private goal of profit for its
members. From the start, the legal personality of the early corporation

was conditional on a clear public regarding role in promoting economic development (or some other public good), and in return investors began effectively to be able to limit their liability to losses on their investments.

The limitation of liability to the initial purchase of shares was a vital step in ensuring that joint-stock companies could obtain the widest possible market for their initial stock offerings. Initially established by custom and practice, liability was only formally limited by statute in the Limited Liability Act of 1855 and the Joint Stock Companies Act of 1856 in the United Kingdom, and in the various states of the United States over the next 40 years. The ability to effectively shield wealth from claims against corporate liability allowed investment in shares to continue to flourish, although not without early criticisms of the manner in which this also limited the moral responsibilities of owners. From the eighteenth century onwards the limitation of liability was a key mechanism underpinning the growth in size and resources of corporations, allowing them access to disparate and unconsolidated capital to a much greater extent than partnerships.

During the second half of the eighteenth century, corporations were increasingly used by the British government to organize private finance to construct the infrastructure that its growing economy required. The development of the railways acted as a significant spur to increased use of incorporation: the scope of operations and the magnitude of financial capital needed to establish the rail infrastructure was so great as to be beyond the resources of companies still organized as partnerships; indeed the need to raise large amounts of capital, as part of the "railway revolution" stimulated the further growth of corporations on both sides of the Atlantic. With the swift economic expansion of America after 1800, new powerful corporations flourished and began to collude to control emerging markets for new goods and products. At first the federal state was willing to turn a blind-eye to cartel activities, but political opposition to such market rigging led finally in 1890 to the Sherman Anti-Trust act.[13] However, paradoxically this encouraged the development of ever-larger corporations through vertical integration (as single entities rather than trusts), controlling many if not all stages of production and able to reach across the continent to control economic activities. Relying increasingly on internally generated surpluses and the stock market, American corporations became larger and more powerful than any that had preceded them.

The industrial revolution and the advances in technology that followed enhanced the possibilities of organizing large-scale business organizations, but corporations also sponsored and stimulated the development of technologies that further enhanced the possibilities for their expansion. The appliance of science and technological innovation, building on the work of Frederick Taylor and others, revolutionized the manner in which production would be organized in the twentieth century.[14] Taylorism, and the linked organizational logic of Fordism were quickly adopted by corporations across the world. Freed from the traditional and historical economic limitations of Europe, the development of capitalist corporations in America proceeded unfettered. The economies of scale gained by larger corporations, with fixed costs spread over ever increasing production volumes (in part caused by the expanding US domestic market), also allowed significant gains for workers and other non-capital owning groups/classes.[15] By expanding productivity through technology and organization, but at the same time producing a significant rise in the standard of living of its workforce (however precarious such advances might be for individuals), US corporate capitalism laid the foundations for a new period of modern capitalism. Large corporations were able to dominate market sectors (nationally and increasingly globally) on the basis of their technological and organizational advantages.

These organizational advances were enthusiastically taken up on the European continent in the first half of the twentieth century; the pressures of catching up in internationalized markets forced German entrepreneurs to adopt these innovations in corporate organization. In both the countries that would become significant industrial competitors for Anglo-Saxon capitalism, Germany and Japan, the shift to banker-led corporate consolidation continued apace from the late nineteenth century, through two world wars and into the present.[16] While in Germany, the numerous *Mittelstand* (medium sized industrial companies) balanced the power and influence of the larger corporations, in Japan the zaibatsu created vast client networks based on cross-shareholding between corporate elements, smaller sub-contracting firms, and their banks. Although each developed their own particular national approaches, Japanese and German industrialists remained influenced by the basic organizational innovations of US corporate capitalism.

The significance of the US corporation is partly in the manner in which production (or services) is organized and the application of "scientific" management, but also how the entire corporation works, from accounting and personal management to its interactions with partners and the global economy more generally.[17] Moreover, as John Kenneth Galbraith argued, the US corporation in the twentieth century often managed to position itself at the heart of the planning of society, as a crucial element in what he famously referred to as the "technostructure."[18] This is not to say all corporations were the same, only that the largest had a clear potential to embed themselves within the governance mechanisms of modern society, but without any linked political accountability. In the late twentieth and into the twenty-first centuries, this embedding developed a global dimension.

While the expansion of US corporations overseas certainly spurred the development of the modern global corporation, this has not been the only organizational model followed. British and other European firms have also utilized "free-standing" companies as a way to invest and develop business in foreign territories.[19] Indeed, this alternative (less-integrated) mode of cross border organization has remained a significant element even for relatively integrated global corporations. Often "free-standing" companies have been able to combine the advantages of corporate organization, alongside the particularities of their home economy, with the network advantages of a globalized organizational structure. The development of global supply chains leading to what Giovanni Arrighi and his co-authors refer to as "concentration without centralization," is perhaps the defining characteristic of the contemporary large (global) corporation.[20] The combination of divisions, subsidiaries, and contracting "partners" into a chain of production steps, networks built to exploit internationally available resources and services while competing in global markets, has led to the emergence of a range of (global) governance issues to which we will return. Nevertheless, in its most general sense the modern corporation (whatever its nationality) owes much to the development of the American corporation, with separation of ownership and management the most significant element.

In the last 100 years the professional manager has become the key corporate player exercising the rights of the corporate personality on behalf of its owners. Thorstein Veblen referred to this development as the rise of "absentee ownership," where those who interacted with the corporation had no chance of meeting an "owner" (and final beneficiary of corporate profits), and thus were distanced from the power of owner-ship. Drawing a direct parallel with absentee landlords, Veblen wanted to stress the corporation's carelessness of the interests of the small holder, supplier, or customer. He concluded that, in effect, the cor-poration is "a method of collusion and concerted action for the joint conduct of transactions designed to benefit the allied and associated owners at the cost of any whom [its actions] may concern … the joint-stock corporation is a conspiracy of owners."[21] The shareholders seldom have any direct interest in the affairs and practices of the cor-poration beyond its ability to offer a return on investment. Therefore, while certainly formally accountable to the board of directors and through them to the shareholders, a new highly rewarded professional global business class has emerged, that while not necessarily completely separate from owners, nevertheless has great latitude for independent management of the (global) corporation. It is this independence that has sometimes bred corruption, scandal, and illegal activities, and with it, a periodic interest in the activities of this cadre of (international) managers. Indeed, it is the interest in and concern with the behavior of (global) corporations and their management(s) that has exposed the corporate economy to demands for regulation and oversight, and the shift to a more globalized system has added a global political dimension to such demands. However, before exploring this set of issues, there are some misapprehensions that we need to clear up.

Terminological exactitude, the retention of national characteristics, and the size of (global) corporations

There are three aspects of the treatment of the global corporation that I want to quickly deal with before moving on. Firstly, I am unsympathetic to the term *transnational* corporation, preferring (and in this book using) the term *global* or multinational corporation(s). It may seem like a little bit of academic vanity but it is as well to be clear in the terms we use and it seems to me that a *transnational* corporation would be one which for all practical purposes transcended nationality both organizationally and culturally. This is to say, a truly *transnational* corporation would have no clearly discernible and continuing link to a particular national history (or set of cultural markers) and would be unlikely therefore to have an organizational center. There are very few globally active corporations that might be regarded as exhibiting this sort of character, and thus I prefer to use the more accurate term *global* corporation: global corporations may have a *global* reach but they are not independent of the international economic system and its continued patterning by (albeit porous) state borders and national legal forms. The *global* corporation works across a multitude of national economies, its management see the market it functions in as being (at least potentially) global but it retains characteristics and legal forms that can be located within the international system not outside it. Certainly some global corporations may seek to transcend the international economic system, but as yet none seem to have managed it (although the case of Apple's tax affairs does raise some interesting issues, see Chapter 5); for instance, as *The Economist* notes, most chief executive officers (which is to say around 75 percent) share the nationality of the corporation they head.[22]

Indeed, this failure to transcend the state is also reflected in the varying cultures and characters of corporations. It is a truism that no two corporations are the same, but equally as a group they share few characteristics beyond the relatively abstract; they are legally defined entities, of which more below; and they are intended to produce a profit (or surplus) on their economic activities. Some years ago Paul Doremus and his co-authors sought to reject the "myth of the global corporation" by examining the range of national foundations for the corporate activity.[23] Quite apart from the national political context, which is related to the notion that there are varieties of capitalism based on national histories of economic development, they identified three key areas by which national forms of corporate behavior or activity might be identified.[24] Firstly, different national histories have shaped the manner in which corporations are governed and the manner in which they organize the capital to fund their operations.[25] Here national legal systems as well as the particular structure of the domestic financial sector (and its relation to global finance), shape the specifics of corporate organizational logics and thereby have some effect on the manner in which corporations attend to these issues and the economic practices they adopt. Alongside these particularities, Doremus and his collaborators suggest that specific national (and historical) practices also shape how corporations organize innovation (the sorts of innovation systems in which they sit), as well as prompting discernibly different approaches to extending their operations through foreign direct investment.[26] There continue to be significant and continuing elements that shape corporations in relation to their national origins and histories.

Therefore, there may be clear and relatively easily identified parallels between corporations from particular countries (or groups of countries), but crucially there is no single (even if relatively general) model for the global corporation. However, global corporations also need to be alive to national or regional differences because these variations in the economies into which they seek to expand their operations may shape the manner, most effective character, and success of their non-domestic investments.[27] This is to say, global corporations increasingly have both national characteristics *and* a global identity, and may seek to operate how they would at home even where legal and regulatory models abroad diverge from those which operate in their home jurisdictions.[28] This can lead to the convergence of practices and behaviors both as corporations seek to establish standard global operating procedures that fulfill varying legal requirements, but also as states seek to establish the regulatory environment that the most powerful (and global) corporations prefer (an issue to which we will return). Thus, in this book while treating global corporations as a group of relatively similar actors, I caution that when applying our analysis of the general to any particular case of corporations' interaction with global governance, we should remain sensitive to the particularities of the case at hand.

Moreover, if the corporation may be less *transnational* than some presentations have suggested (or at least imply), it is as well also to be a little skeptical about their size, especially when measurements of size are translated (often crudely and directly) into an assessment of their political power. Firstly, the comparison of gross domestic product (GDP) and annual turnover of corporations is an often encountered juxtaposition,[29] but this does not compare like with like: while GDP is a measure of the value-added of a national economy in a year, the sales or turnover figures of corporations are just that; sales figures, which while including value-added are an aggregated figure in the way GDP is not.[30] Moreover, while turnover is relatively easy to calculate, GDP is a complex statistical construct subject to shifts and methodological changes much more profound than corporate accounts.[31] Thus, if we assume that global corporate economic activity might on average add around 25 percent of value to the resources deployed, this suggests that crude comparisons overstate the comparable size of national economies and corporations by around four times.[32] Even the World Bank makes this fundamental error, claiming in a chart from 2009 (and still on the website) that Royal Dutch Shell (RDS) (ranked 32nd in a global list of The World's Top 100 Economies) is bigger than Egypt, Pakistan, and Belgium, to pick three countries from just below its place in the table.[33] These figures are then used by campaigning groups to assess the political power of these organizations, and to suggest that "something must be done."[34] However, even if one accepted the translation of size into power, noting the argument about measuring the same thing, a quick recalculation takes RDS from 32nd to a level well below the 100th rated "economy" in the World Bank's figures.

Another way of looking at the size of global corporations is to compare the sales figures of a global corporation (less its profit which will be distributed to shareholders and a proportion paid to the state via tax, with only some re-invested) with the effective budgets of states (rather than national GDP figures). This at least compares things that are broadly similar; in both cases this approximates the level of economic activity of the entity by virtue of the money deployed/spent on its activities.[35] Thus, for instance, the United Kingdom in 2013/14 budgeted to spend £720 billion while RDS' effective sales figure in 2012 was around £280 billion (net of profit and taxes), giving perhaps a more plausible comparison of economic weight, although equally it should be recalled that RDS' budget was spread across all its international activity while the bulk of the UK state's expenditure takes place within the borders of the country. Alternatively, sometimes market capitalization is preferred as a measure of size (with the implication this might have some impact on a corporation's political influence), although this would be dwarfed by any account of all assets (land; infrastructure and so on) held by any specific country (which would be the fair comparison). *The Economist* often ranks firms by capitalization and allocates them to home countries to suggest, in its figures for 2013, that the largest firms were once again (after a time when other nationalities vied for the top ten) almost all US multinationals, concluding that therefore the United States was "winning" some form of global competition.[36]

Perhaps the key thing to stress here is that a simplistic reading across this sort of comparable data to reach conclusions about political power is not particularly satisfactory. In Chapter 4, I come back to the issue of the power of global corporations and how we might recognize how (and if) this is being exercised, after also touching on this issue in the chapter that follows this Introduction. Finally, not all multinational corporations operating in a number of national jurisdictions and between them, are necessarily of the scale of those largest corporations often listed in the tables of most significant global economic entities; there are plenty, indeed the vast majority, that while multinational may for all intents and purposes be relatively small companies when compared with Apple, General Motors, or the oil companies. This book is just as much about them as the leviathans of the global corporate sector, even if sometimes they are less visible.

The importance of corporate legal form(s)

Finally, before setting out the overall shape of the argument that I will be making in the subsequent chapters, I want to stress the importance of an appreciation of the legal aspects of the corporation. Although I will return to the central issue of its legal personality later, as it is difficult to appreciate the political economy of global corporations and the relation with global governance without an initial appreciation of the role of the legal form, here I will briefly highlight some salient issues that will help contextualize the argument developed in the next few chapters.

Although corporations are organizations made up of groups of people, various social and internal institutions, and capital (and other) assets mobilized towards a set of economic (and sometime extra-economic) ends, they are usually treated as having a single personality for legal purposes. This pays clear organizational dividends within contract law for instance: the corporation can be dealt with as an effective signatory to agreements and undertakings. As would be inferred from the discussion of the national differences between corporate characteristics, there is no single and universal legal form for global corporations. However, although there are many other modes of corporate organization, the central aspects of the Anglo-Saxon legal form have become increasingly influential and widespread in the new millennium, especially as regards legal personality. Moreover, for many corporations the desire (or need) to compete to raise capital in London or New York, and thus seek stock market listings in the United Kingdom or United States, has a significant impact on the adoption of specific legal arrangements to deliver specified accounting and financial reporting requirements.[37] Through compliance with such regulations, this particular legal form has been exported to countries with differing legal traditions and practices. This partial convergence of corporate forms has not necessarily been beneficial for the accountability of business; the increasing adoption of Anglo-Saxon modes of limited liability within the governance of subsidiaries has shielded companies and their shareholders from accountability across their international networks. This is partly the result of another key element of the corporate legal form; the ability to hold stock (or own) other companies;[38] like "real" individuals, corporations are often legally able to hold stock in other corporations (or their own "subsidiaries") allowing the company itself to benefit from the protection of limited liability (originally formulated to protect *individuals* from excessive risk not corporations themselves), in its role as a holding company.

I will be examining the legal personality of the corporation at some length in Chapter 2, but it is worth (again) noting that the assumption of legal personality through incorporation was a grant of authority by the state to carry out certain purposes for the public good. In the seventeenth century when this first became widely used, these public purposes were defined by the state with relatively little public participation or deliberation, but nevertheless were framed as public interests and constraining rights to private enrichment. Perhaps the key shift in the political appreciation of incorporation has been a move from a conception of delegation of certain powers from the state, to seeing it as a mode of protection from the state.[39] Thus, now that the (multinational) corporation stands before us, with its supporters arguing that its forms and practices are not political but merely technical, we are confronted with the question of how far such corporations actually do fulfill their side of any (now forgotten) bargain.[40] Underlying much of the argument of this book, is the argument that the treatment of the corporation as legally constituted individual, and the assumption that it necessarily contributes to economic well-being needs to be subjected to scrutiny and democratic deliberation if business and democracy are to be reconciled within a nascent global society, and subjected to a legitimate form of global governance.

We know that most corporations do not have the institutional longevity of (most) established states, nevertheless their enjoyment of legal personality (and the attendant rights of that personality) allows them to deploy considerably greater social power than the natural persons on whose rights these corporate rights are often modeled. Just to be clear, three distinct legal personalities are generally recognized in law: naturally existing people (that is, individuals in a particular jurisdiction); the state (in its role as collective location of sovereign and legal authority); and the legally constituted corporation, a collective organization recognized for the purposes of regulation as having a single legal personality. This division is hardly natural, and while the division between (sovereign) political authority and individual subject (or later citizen) might be said to have emerged almost organically from the historical and legal requirements of nation-state politics, the assumption of legal personhood by the corporation was a politically engineered legal innovation.

As Steve Russell and Michael Gilbert have pointed out: "Corporations have many advantages over natural persons: effective immortality, superior resources, and with globalization, mobility on a scale available to few human beings."[41] Thus, the divergence between the legal protection available to all (legally constituted) people, and the different effective position of the various types of individuals claiming the protection of the law has been central to much critical discussion of modern corporations. While corporations remain outside the scope of international law, like other persons they are subjects only of national law, corporations' recourse to legalized personality is a relatively internationalized legal structure even if it remains a national jurisdictional matter. While corporations may be influenced by international "soft law," little regulation at the international level has been solidified into (hard) positive law to hold them firmly to account outside national jurisdictions.[42] This has the advantage of offering corporations opportunities for organizational convergence with its posited associated efficiency benefits, but with few of the accountability costs of formal legislative development.

This *does* mean that multinational corporations are exposed to a significant legal tension: they are constituted under the laws of their home country, and as such (as noted above) this will have some impact on their character and practices. However, equally most countries require the local subsidiary operation of any corporation to be constituted under local (national) law, and as such, frequently a global multinational's legal form is highly diversified. This can lead to an attempt by governments of multinationals' home/head-quarters states to seek to extend their legal reach (the extraterritoriality of their regulatory focus) through demands that local subsidiaries should be governed by the regulations of the home country even if these conflict with those of the subsidiary's host jurisdiction.[43] Conversely, host states may also seek to hold multinationals accountable through national legal mechanisms which may be in tension with how the corporation expects to manage its affairs in its head-quarters (home) country. Where bilateral investment treaties (BITs) have been negotiated, the host state may end up constricting its own ability to so regulate as a way of "encouraging" inwards investment, of which more later. The corporation is therefore a creature of the law, albeit with multiple (legal) parents; it is this question of how the corporation exists as a legal entity in the global political economy that in one sense lies at the heart of everything that follows.

The rest of the book

In the next chapter I set out in relatively broad terms the aspects of global governance that will concern much of the analysis in the rest of the book. I explore both how global corporations are subject to various elements of global governance (introducing a couple of key examples including the World Trade Organization), and also briefly set out some general points about how and why the global corporate sector collectively, or particular corporations individually, might try to influence the agenda of contemporary global governance (linked to their interest in market share and profits). At the end of the chapter I introduce the idea that corporations may be institutions of global governance themselves, both through their standards setting activities and by virtue of the control over the political economic interactions within their extended networks. The key point of the chapter is to stress that global corporations feel the effects of global governance in various ways (and to various degrees) and as such, given their developed diplomatic function we should be unsurprised that they seek to influence and shape the modes of governance they confront in their everyday activities.

In Chapter 2 I focus on the legal personality of the corporation as a key element in understanding its (global) political economy. I begin by setting out the distinction between natural persons and legally constituted persons, before moving to discuss perhaps the most significant aspect of a corporation's legal personality, its enjoyment of the benefits of limited liability. I then examine how we might understand the corporate legal person as a citizen enjoying certain rights and benefits available from its host state. While at times this chapter may seem not to be about global governance, the issues it explores are vital if we are to work towards an understanding of the relationship between global corporations and the institutions of global governance that goes beyond a simplified notion of business interests. In the next two chapters I then ask how we might understand global governance's interaction with the internal governance of corporations, before then asking how corporations exercise power in the realm of global governance.

Therefore, in Chapter 3 I focus on the shape and forms of corporate governance, starting with an overview of the wide range of issues of corporate governance that are the focus of legal and regulatory attention, leading me to contrast the interests of owners and managers. Having discussed one dimension of the governance of corporate practices, essentially focused on the board of directors, I then briefly discuss corporate social responsibility (CSR), how this is articulated through the UN Global Compact (the nearest thing to a global governance mechanism regulating CSR), and conclude by returning to the essential voluntary character of regulatory regimes around CSR contrasted with more formalized regimes where these are "required" by the global corporate sector. Chapter 4 explores the key issue of how we can understand global corporate power in the realm of global governance, starting with a brief contextual discussion of the analysis of power more generally (relating this to corporations) before focusing on the issue of how this might play out in global governance. The key element of this discussion is the requirement that an analysis of (global) corporate power does not limit itself to the mobilization of the myriad resources available to the corporate sector but also includes recognition of the role of discursive power and the ability to shape the agendas of decision. The chapter concludes with a brief discussion of the corporation as an institution of global governance itself, drawing together a number of threads from previous chapters. The analysis set out in this chapter is then deployed in the next chapter to explain the contemporary global governance regime around global corporate taxation; here the role of corporate power seems to have been to contribute to the lack of development of a formalized governance structure. Thus, Chapter 5 develops a case study that combines the elements developed in previous chapters to explore the relationship between global governance and global corporations.

The final chapter briefly reviews the complex relations between global corporations over three dimensions: the impact of global governance on global corporations; the influence of global corporations on global governance; and the issue of whether we might usefully also think of global corporations as institutions of global governance themselves. As this final chapter suggests, this book has been an attempt to explore the wide terrain over which an account of specific global corporations' relationship with particular elements of global governance would need to range. As such, for readers interested in this relationship what I offer here is a starting point for detailed research rather than firm conclusions about the manner in which global corporations and global governance interact.

Notes

1 Ambrose Bierce, *The Devil's Dictionary* (Neal Publishing [reprinted, New York: Dover Publications] 1911 [1958]), 25.
2 *The Economist*, "Free Exchange: The humble hero," 18 May 2013, 74.
3 Karl Moore and David Lewis, *Birth of the Multinational: 2000 Years of Ancient Business History – from Ashur to Augustus* (Copenhagen: Copenhagen Business School Press, 1999).
4 Samuel Williston, "The History of the Law of Business Corporations before 1800" in *Select Essays in Anglo-American Legal History* (Volume III) ed. Association of American Law Schools (Cambridge: Cambridge University Press 1909), 197.
5 Bruce Brown, *The History of the Corporation* (Volume One) (Sumas, Wash.: BF Communications 2003).
6 John P. Davis, *Corporations. A Study of the Origin and Development of Great Business Combinations and of their Relation to the Authority of the State* (New York: G.P. Putnam's Sons, 1905).
7 Colin Arthur Cooke, *Corporation, Trust and Company: An Essay in Legal History* (Manchester: Manchester University Press 1950), 183.
8 Ibid., 31, 39
9 Geoffrey Jones, *Merchants to Multinationals: British Trading Companies in the Nineteenth and Twentieth Centuries* (Oxford: Oxford University Press 2000).
10 Dennis M.P. McCarthy, *International Business History. A Contextual and Case Approach* (Westport, Conn.: Praeger, 1994).
11 Davis, *Corporations* (Vol. II), 210.
12 Williston, "The History of the Law of Business Corporations before 1800," 201.
13 Richard Kozul-Wright, "The Myth of Anglo-Saxon Capitalism: Reconstructing the History of the American State" in *The Role of the State in Economic Change*, ed. H.J. Chang and R. Rowthorn (Oxford: Clarendon Press, 1995), 104.
14 David F. Noble, *America by Design. Science, Technology and the Rise of Corporate Capitalism* (Oxford: Oxford University Press, 1977).

15 Stephen Resnick and Richard Wolff, "Exploitation, Consumption and the Uniqueness of US Capitalism," *Historical Materialism* 11, no. 4 (2003): 209–226.

16 John Micklethwait, and Adrian Wooldridge, *The Company. A Short History of a Revolutionary Idea* (London: Weidenfeld and Nicolson, 2003), 83–101.

17 Noble, *America by Design.*

18 John Kenneth Galbraith, *The New Industrial Staten* (fourth edition with a new introduction) (Boston, Mass.: Houghton Mifflin Co, 1985).

19 Mira Wilkins, and Harm Schröter eds, *The Free-Standing Company in the World Economy, 1830–1996* (Oxford: Oxford University Press, 1998).

20 Giovanni Arrighi, Kenneth Barr, and Shuji Hisaeda, "The Transformation of Business Enterprise" in *Chaos and Governance in the Modern World System*, ed. G. Arrighi and B.J. Silver (Minneapolis: University of Minnesota Press, 1999), 149.

21 Thorstein Veblen, *Absentee Ownership. Business Enterprise in Recent Times: The Case of America* (New York: B.W. Heubsch [reprinted with a new introduction by Marion J Levy. New Brunswick, N.J.: Transaction Publishers], 1923 [1997]), 409.

22 *The Economist*, "Schumpeter: Bumpkin bosses," 10 May 2014, 69.

23 Paul Doremus, William W. Keller, Louis W. Pauly, and Simon Reich, *The Myth of the Global Corporation* (Princeton, N.J.: Princeton University Press, 1998).

24 See: Peter A. Hall, and David Soskice, eds, *Varieties of Capitalism. The Institutional Foundations of Comparative Advantage* (Oxford: Oxford University Press, 2001), but compare, Alan Rugman and Alain Verbeke, "The Regional Dimension of Multinationals and the End of 'Varieties of Capitalism'" in *The Images of the Multinational Firm*, ed. S. Collinson and G. Morgan (Chichester: John Wiley & Sons, 2009): 23–44.

25 Doremus *et al.*, *Myth of the Global Corporation*, Chapter 3.

26 Ibid., Chapter 4.

27 Rugman and Verbeke, "The Regional Dimension of Multinationals," 38; Stephen Wilks, "The National Identity of Global Companies" in *The Handbook of Global Companies*, ed. J. Mikler (Chichester: John Wiley & Sons 2013), 44–45.

28 Ibid., 49.

29 For instance, Hinrich Vos, "The Global Company" in *The Handbook of Global Companies*, ed. J. Mikler (Chichester: John Wiley & Sons 2013), 22–23; D. Eleanor Westney, "The Multinational Firm as an Evolutionary System" in *The Images of the Multinational Firm*, ed. S. Collinson and G. Morgan (Chichester: John Wiley & Sons 2009), 122.

30 Jagdish Bhagwati, *In Defense of Globalization* (New Delhi: Oxford University Press, 2004), 166; *World Investment Report 2002: Transnational Corporations and Export Competitiveness* (New York: United Nations Conference on Trade and Development, 2002), 90.

31 See the extensive discussion in Diane Coyle, *GDP: A brief but affectionate history* (Princeton, N.J.: Princeton University Press, 2014), which demonstrates that GDP is not a reliable comparator for other metrics.

32 Graeme Thompson, "Globalisation as the Total Commercialisation of Politics?," *New Political Economy* 8, no. 3 (2003), 407.

33 See: World Bank *World's Top 100 Economies.* http://siteresources.worldban
    k.org/INTUWM/Resources/WorldsTop100Economies.pdf.
34 See Oxfam's *From Poverty to Power* blog from two years later – www.
    oxfamblogs.org/fp2p/?p=7164.
35 Jeff Harrod "The Century of the Corporation" *Global Corporate Power*
    (IPE Yearbook 15), ed. C. May (Boulder, Colo.: Lynne Rienner Publishers,
    2006), 24.
36 *The Economist*, "Briefing: The world's biggest firms," 21 September 2013:
    24–25.
37 Henry Hansmann and Reinier Kraakman, *The End of History for Corpo-
    rate Law* (Yale Law School: Law and Economics Working Paper no. 235)
    (New Haven, Conn.: Yale Law School, 2000).
38 Peter T. Muchlinski, *Multilateral Enterprises and the Law* (second edition)
    (Oxford: Oxford University Press, 2007), 35.
39 Sol Picciotto, *Regulating Global Corporate Capitalism: International Cor-
    porate Law and Financial Market Regulation* (Cambridge: Cambridge
    University Press, 2011), 113.
40 Joel Bakan, *The Corporation: The Pathological Pursuit of Profit and Power*
    (New York: Free Press, 2004).
41 Steve Russell and Michael J. Gilbert, "Social Control of Transnational
    Corporations in the Age of Marketocracy," *International Journal of the
    Sociology of the Law* 30 (March 2002), 45.
42 Muchlinski, *Multilateral Enterprises and the Law*, 111.
43 Stephen J. Kobrin, "Sovereignty@Bay: Globalization, Multinational
    Enterprise and the International Political System" in *The Oxford Hand-
    book of International Business* (second edition), ed. A.M. Rugman (Oxford:
    Oxford University Press, 2009), 189–190.

1 Global corporations and global governance

- Governing the global corporate sector
- Shaping the agenda of global governance
- Global corporations as institutions of global governance themselves
- Conclusion

Having introduced the global corporation, this chapter maps the general terrain where the more focused issues raised in subsequent chapters are located and as such introduces a number of key themes of the book. The idea of global governance itself is of relatively recent vintage; the term seeks to capture the move from an international system, ruled by the direct and relatively unmediated activities of powerful states, to one where politics is understood globally, with many more actors than just states actively seeking to affect political change. To speak of the "global" is to move away from understanding political power mainly as territorially defined, and towards a recognition that power in global politics is not merely an attribute of states, with "governance" a shorthand for international influence and authority located outside state institutions. This also reflects the gradual development of powerful legally grounded international organizations, starting in the nineteenth century with a focus on the regulation of international communications and (some) economic affairs.[1] The range and number of these institutions of international law accelerated during the years of the League of Nations and more so after the establishment of the United Nations, until the complexity and number of institutions prompted the identification of a specific set of practices and range of attributes that we now most often refer to as global governance.

Given the roots of contemporary global governance in the nineteenth century's period of rapid economic globalization, it should be no surprise that businesses have always been interested in the form and content of the rules and regulations that emerged from the state-led negotiations establishing various regimes intended to oversee particular (often economic) issue areas. Certainly, governments have consulted (sometimes formally, sometimes informally) with business leaders and representatives when developing and then interacting with international institutions especially where, as is often the case, the institutions are likely to have some impact on international (and now, global) economic relations. However, there are, of course, disagreements about how we should understand the character of the interaction between global governance institutions, states' governments and corporations: some commentators see corporations' role as potentially constructive, as in the recent moves against bribery and corruption,[2] whereas others see corporations presenting problems for the democratic accountability of these institutions.[3]

Whatever one's assessment of the character of these interactions, it is difficult to argue that a study of contemporary global governance need take no account of the corporate sector (and few nowadays would take that position). Indeed for organizations like the International Labor Organization, founded in 1919, the business sector has always been involved in developing regulatory measures and practices. As globalization accelerated after the end of the Cold War, the scope of multinational corporations' activities and the focus of many international institutions became increasingly aligned, offering further incentives for both to engage the other in discussion and negotiation.[4] Therefore, while the global business sector may now be more organized than it was before the Second World War, this is not to suggest that international businesses were absent from the realm of international rule making before their role in the development of global governance became a matter for critical comment. Thus, as I will begin to show below, global governance now clearly encompasses at least four distinct interactive sets of actors: states; the institutions of global governance themselves; non-governmental organizations focused on global activity (whose role is covered by other books in this series and only a minor element of the analysis here); *and* multinational or global corporations.

Although it is some time since John Stopford and Susan Strange set out an account which sought to situate corporations individually or collectively within the international diplomatic realm, their analysis makes a useful point about the global corporate sector.[5] They presented corporations as fully rounded non-state actors that have legitimate interests, interacting with states, the institutions of global governance and other actors or groups active in the global realm on a number of levels and around a range of issues. States' governments have increasingly put economic growth at the center of their policy agendas seeking to claim their expertise and success in growth as a key reason for their continued democratic legitimacy; unsurprisingly this has prompted an expansion of states' involvement and engagement with the private corporate sector. However, Stopford and Strange's argument that this therefore implied an expanded *partnership* between states and corporations has to some extent been eroded in the quarter century since their study was originally published.

Certainly, states have entered (political) alliances with multinational and smaller, local corporations to deliver market share and capital accumulation to the corporation with a clear overall intent to contribute towards domestic economic growth. These alliances have ranged from the weak links of positive legislative support (laws that favor business development in one way or another) to more developed partnerships (ranging from outsourcing of government activity to direct financial support). However, the continuing development of more open global markets (partly the result of state actions and policies themselves) has also continued to move elements of the governance of this activity away from single national jurisdictions to international organizations with varying levels of oversight and authority, prompting further fragmentation; additionally the Internet has increased the potential for individuals and groups to mobilize political campaigns against corporate actions at the global rather than national level.[6] In response, global corporations have adopted a more globalized form of diplomatic function in their relations with states, global governance institutions, and (global) civil society, contributing to (and shaping) global governance itself, while also responding and accommodating new global rules and guidance as regards their operations across the world. It is to these two diplomatic functions we now turn as they are the context for much of the discussion in subsequent chapters.

Governing the global corporate sector

Although it might seem obvious that global governance affects the practice and activities of global corporations, it is as well to be explicit about the general manner in which global governance helps shape and direct their behavior. Although recent developments in international criminal law have expanded the subjects of international law to include (some) individuals, in the main international law (which underpins global governance) has only included states as the subjects of law; thus corporations mostly only have international legal personality as nationals of states. Nevertheless, even though states are international law's immediate subjects, corporations' activities are subject to a myriad of regulations established through a wide range global governance institutions and, as such, there is considerable debate about the extent of corporations' exposure to international legal instruments,[7] to which we return in the next chapter. These regulations have not necessarily been forced onto corporations, rather as global corporations' operations have become more complex and *global* their senior management teams have often sought action in the international arena from their home states to establish a more ordered and standardized environment for economic activity.[8] Thus the impact of global governance on the corporation can be both facilitative of its economic activity and/or represent a constraint on corporations' preferred activity.

Many regulations directly related to the global corporate sector find their origins in the earlier bilateral investment, trade promotion, and property rights protection treaties stretching back in some instances to the nineteenth century.[9] These agreements mostly sought to harmonize legal and regulatory instruments between home and host countries involved in significant bilateral economic relations, and such treaties have continued to be negotiated into the new millennium, with around 2800 bilateral investment treaties (BITs) in force by 2010.[10] These treaties are complemented by various international and regional investment agreements, as well as the regulations of the World Trade Organization (of which more below). However, while related to corporate activity, the key focus of investment agreements is the curtailment of expropriations (often nationalization) of corporate property. Such agreements have aimed to limit the freedom of host states to interfere with foreign owned corporate property while also providing for arbitration when such expropriation does happen.[11] Such arbitration seeks to settle the compensation or damages owed to the investor (or investing corporation) by the state when property has been "taken" by the state, including the national treatment of non-domestic corporations— foreign corporations should be treated no worse than domestic firms in a similar situation—with much of the case law in these cases favoring the corporate perception of levels of loss.

However, corporations can also have their actions regulated (directly, or more often indirectly) in areas of activity other than direct investment and trading; one important example is the impact on corporate practices of the various climate change governance regimes of which the Kyoto Protocol is likely the most important but not only the mechanism requiring amendments to practice in light of their impact on the environment (usually mediated through state level laws). Another example is the regulation of the international banking industry through the Basel Committee on Banking Supervision, which is an organ of the Group of 10 developed countries and has its roots in the funding arrangements of the International Monetary Fund, bringing together Belgium, Canada, France, Italy, Japan, the Netherlands, the United Kingdom, the United States, Germany, Sweden, and Switzerland (the latter joining a couple of years after the group was launched in 1964, but not reflected in the group's name).

In addition to these focused (and binding) agreements, global corporations are subject to a number of multilateral treaties that offer guidelines and expectations rather than enforceable rules. These include the Organization for Economic Cooperation and Development (OECD) Guidelines for Multinational Enterprises (adopted in 1976 and most recently revised in 2011), and the UN Global Compact (see below and Chapter 3). Alongside these general sets of guidelines there are various standards organizations with industrial sector related, or an issue area focus which also seek to regulate corporate behavior in various ways. Organizations working with guidelines often involve a range of stakeholders seeking to govern or control the behavior of corporations around specific politically sensitive issues, for instance involving the environment or labor and employment practices or corporations' impact on host country's economic development. Here, governance can be relatively weak with a lack of formal enforceable constraints only partly balanced by the power of normative engagement, and the sanction of publicity, with questions of verification and "real" corporate commitment to codes offering critical weaknesses that are difficult to resolve.[12] As the above indicates, there is an extensive and mixed ecology of regulatory institutions of global governance that potentially have some impact on global corporations' day-to-day activities.

To explore this in a little more detail with a couple of examples, let's start with the World Trade Organization (WTO), not least as it is often central to accounts of global governance. The WTO is an important regulator of a number of aspects of the global political economy of relevance to global corporations, not least of all as much global trade flows through global corporations; by some measures intra-firm and inter-firm trade account for the vast majority (around two-thirds) of all international trade.[13] The WTO's primary concern is to open up markets to freer competition, and thus one key focus of its activity which impacts on corporations operating in any members' jurisdiction is the progressive reduction in barriers to international competition in domestic markets by reducing import tariffs and other impediments. Additionally, there are four specific areas of concern to corporations' management, and for each we can identify aspects of the WTO regulatory regime that have some impact on decisions about corporate practices and activities.

i *Location of production*: national treatment as a norm—non-national corporations must be treated no worse than local firms (and of course can be treated better)—via the WTO's principle of non-discrimination; the General Agreement on Services (GATS) (related particularly to national procurement practices); and provisions of the Trade Related Investment Measures (TRIMs) agreement.

ii *Access to markets*: the general provisions of the WTO; more specifically, GATS as related to non-product markets for services; the reduction of tariffs; the reduction of barriers to imports (the removal of localized regulations, regarded as discriminatory by the WTO).

iii *Structure of industries*: the reduction of subsidies; procurement practices again.

iv *Management of corporate functions*: the protection of intellectual property under the Trade Related Aspects of Intellectual Property Rights (TRIPs) agreement, as regards corporate resources (and their "location"); the regulation and facilitation of technology transfer (TRIPs); GATS relating to visas for personnel moving around international corporate structures.[14]

As this indicates, there are a wide range of areas where the WTO has some impact on how corporations manage and develop their international activities (from investment, to internal management of the organization). However, that impact can be widely different across different elements of the WTO's "single undertaking" (by which state members accede to *all* aspects of the WTO's regulatory complex).

For instance, while the TRIPs agreement is relatively strong in its shaping of permissible corporate activity, the Subsidies and Countervailing Measures (SCM) agreement is both weaker in terms of its enforcement and much less focused in policy terms.[15] Thus, although there have been considerable political confrontations about the limitations on emerging market corporations that the TRIPs agreement has instituted (most obviously around the re-use of technologies), the SCM agreement has had relatively little impact on corporations' ability to request and be granted subsidies (and other forms of support) right across the WTO's membership from the most developed to the least developed states. The TRIPs agreement has relatively precise legislative demands (and indeed is the only WTO element that requires changes

in *domestic* laws not merely laws effecting cross-border activity), while
the SCM agreement includes such extensive latitude for governments
and the corporations with whom they have allied to support economic
development, that the relatively low level of sanction (linked merely to
claimed economic impact on the complainant member) has allowed
states (and their corporate allies) to treat the WTO's sanctions as a
price for breaching the SCM agreement, if and when a complaint is
lodged.[16] Even within a single organization the shape and form of
impact of global governance on corporations can vary by issue area.

There are a wide range of other organizations that have a narrower
impact on activities. For instance, the International Accounting Standards Board (IASB) has been able to promulgate standardized
accounting methods for corporate assets, introducing and supporting
the "fair value" approach. Here values of corporations' assets are
delinked from their historical costs (and issues of depreciation of value
over time), with values now assessed against current market values (or
proxies)—so-called marking-to-market. Once the European Union had
made the IASB's International Financial Reporting Standards (IFRS)
binding on all publicly listed corporations in the EU, with other jurisdictions (with the initial exception of the United States) taking a
similar line, corporations were subject to (and mostly welcomed) a
broadly comprehensive regime of governance regarding their financial
reporting.[17] In a different issue area, international air transport is
regulated through the International Air Transport Association (IATA),
an international trade association (whose members currently account
for over 80 percent of all civilian air traffic)—for economic issues—and
the International Civil Aviation Organization (ICAO), a specialized
agency of the UN—for technical issues. Successive rounds of privatization of previously nationalized carriers and deregulation have
reduced the cartel-like power of IATA to regulate fares and conditions,
moving its role towards guidance although still representing an (albeit
softer) governance effect. However, as one might expect the major air-
frame manufacturers—Boeing and Airbus—still play a major role in
the ICAO, while the organization itself remains dominated by state
interests, and most powerfully the interests of the United States whose
airlines continue to be major players in the sector.[18] Recent developments have seen a move to a more multi-stakeholder approach and,
not least through the investigative response to accidents, a ratcheting
up of performance standards (and a shift away from specification
standards) which has had clear safety pay-offs for the general public
and not merely for the reputations of the corporations involved in the
industry.

Moving from governance mechanisms related to specific policy or issues areas to the everyday conduct of corporations, here guidance and voluntary codes are most evident with little direct *international* legal constraint on activities (although, of course, all corporations remain subject to the law of the states in which they operate). In 1976 the OECD adopted its Guidelines for Multinational Enterprises (which in its 2011 edition runs to 95 pages). While highly detailed the Guidelines are focused on either avoiding, or at least ameliorating, adverse social impacts of global corporations, activities in a range of issue areas, including transparent organizational practices (termed "disclosure"), human rights, employment and industrial relations, the environment, corruption of various sorts, consumer interests, technology transfer, competition, and taxation.[19] The OECD also obliges its member states to promote the observance of the guidelines by corporations based in their countries,[20] but of course this limits its scope to those corporations who are incorporated in one or other of the 34 (current) members of the OECD. Whatever one's assessment of the efficacy of this code, with outsourcing and the fragmentation of corporate supply chains (into complex global networks including many independent suppliers), there are many corporations that can perfectly legitimately see aspects of their activities at least partly outside the scope of these guidelines.

Therefore, still utilizing non-formal regulation, but seeking to encompass the entire global political economy, the United Nations has attempted to establish some regulatory oversight of global corporate practices. Following a speech by the UN secretary general at the World Economic Forum the previous year, in 2000 the UN Global Compact was launched. Reflecting the increasingly prevalent practice of public-private partnership, the UN Global Compact is organized on the basis of reputational incentives and benchmarks, a set of carrots rather than sticks; it encompasses a set of principles that have been developed in the public realm but are to be enacted privately. The compact is intended to place human rights, labor standards, "environmental stewardship," and the reduction of corruption at the center of corporations' practices and planning. Rather than offering a code-of-conduct, the compact offers, as George Kell and John Ruggie (its chief architects) note, "a framework of reference and dialogue to stimulate best practice and to bring about convergence in corporate practices around universally shared values."[21] Corporations are asked to adopt the compact, integrate the values it expresses into their mission statements and management practices, and regularly report on their progress towards fulfilling the aims of the compact itself; the only firm commitment they need to make is to supply information about their behavior. Many corporations now seem to recognize that questions regarding human rights can have a direct impact on their financial well-being, through the practices and decisions of the corporation itself, and through pressure brought to bear on management by a diverse set of shareholders, stakeholders, and regulators. However, it is not only in the area of human rights that corporations have been encouraged by the Global Compact to become better "citizens."

As Ruggie has noted, the Global Compact is a "social learning network [that] operates on the premise that socially legitimated good practices will help drive out bad ones through the power of transparency and competition."[22] This voluntary approach reflects a presumption that it would prove difficult, if not impossible to generate a robust multilateral code of conduct for corporations; that the compact may be all that it is presently possible to achieve. It is intended to peg corporate behavior to internationally recognized "best practice," and thus may allow some "ratcheting up" of standards, related to its nine principles.[23] The compact itself was originally conceived as a relatively small contribution to the general aim of changing the practices of corporations, but as it has developed, more weight has been laid on its ability to affect significant change by itself.[24] The formal adoption of the compact allows corporations, in theory at least, to be held to account through the surveillance of civil society groups.

Anne-Marie Slaughter therefore regards the compact as exemplary of a new form of horizontal government, where sovereign authorities now facilitate self-regulation through the conduct of deliberative and formative forums, rather than directly regulating.[25] Indeed, Kell and Ruggie suggested on its establishment that global corporations would be attracted to the compact precisely because it is voluntary, offering

> one stop shopping in the three critical areas of greatest external pressure, human rights, environment and labor standards, thereby reducing their transactions costs. It offers the legitimacy of having corporations sign off on to something sponsored by the Secretary-General—and, far more important, the legitimacy of acting on universally agreed principles that are enshrined in covenants and declarations.[26]

However, many non-government organizations (NGOs) are less sanguine about the Global Compact. Some (most often the larger, multinational NGOs) see it as an aspect of constructive engagement with the "corporate community," while others (often smaller, single issue

NGOs) see the compact as a pact with the devil, leading to the co-option of previously critical groups into the global corporate project and a diminution of their ability to offer a counter-balance to the corporate interest.

Even initially supportive NGOs have expressed concerns about the weakness of the compact's influence on its signatories' practices.[27] The Global Compact's very character suggests that efforts at more formal control have been undermined by the ability of corporations to mobilize significant resources to compromise political control (or extensive regulation) of their activities. We will examine the compact in the discussion of corporate social responsibility in Chapter 3, but it is useful to note here that one on-going reaction to its perceived failings has been the expansion of what David Vogel has termed "civil regulation," the development of regulatory standards and principles of behavior arising from (global) civil society and organized political campaigns focusing on corporate conduct.[28] Of these campaigns and regulatory developments, likely the most successful has been the regulation of what are now routinely referred to as "conflict diamonds," which has seen the Kimberley Process largely halt the flow of diamonds from guerrilla, militia, and other irregular military groups onto the global market, removing this as a way of funding continuing conflicts.[29] Other less extensive but still moderately effective civil regulatory developments have sought to establish certification of corporate activity in areas such as "fair-trade" labeling, for example enacted in the international coffee market, and the support for sustainable forestry through the Forest Stewardship Council.[30] Responding to perceived publicity effects and issues of brand integrity, some global corporations such as Levis or US Whole Foods have quite significantly shifted their practices (most often related to their supply chain) in response to codes of conduct emanating from civil regulatory organizations.

Conversely, these changes in practice do not seem to have had a major positive *or* negative impact on any particular corporation's profitability or market valuation.[31] As with the Global Compact, there remain some perceptions of a danger that corporations will game the system, or sign-up to codes while only incompletely implementing or embedding them in their day-to-day management. Thus, perhaps unsurprisingly, in 2013 *The Economist* detected disillusionment on both sides; corporations saw their association with various campaigning NGOs as failing to offer them political cover (for instance BP's involvement with environment NGOs did it little good in the oil spill crisis in the Gulf of Mexico), while groups who have worked on clothing supply chains with all the major companies being supplied by factories at Rana Plaza in Bangladesh discovered that they had been unable to protect the lives of workers killed in the building's collapse.[32] We will return to the question of how much such activity around corporate social responsibility (as part of civil regulation) has been able to reshape corporate activity in Chapter 3.

Shaping the agenda of global governance

Having set out in broad terms the extent of global corporations' exposure to global governance, we now move to the issue which for most commentators and analysts is the key concern when considering the relationship between the corporate sector and the institutions of global governance: to what extent do corporations shape the agenda of global governance? Doris Fuchs argues that business groups and individual corporations have for at least three decades recognized the need for the development and deployment of "discursive power," and this power is often deployed in the realm of regulation.[33] Fuchs defines this form of power as the power to (re)define norms and values that serve a particular interest as being emerging or ascendant *general* norms and values, alongside a developed capacity to (re)produce these norms beyond the immediate confines of corporate interrelations. However, while this discursive power may be articulated through the media and other communicative channels (with corporations mobilizing large communications and advertising budgets), global corporations have also sought to establish, or perhaps more accurately maintain, a specific set of narratives around the roots of innovation and economic development through more direct means. Corporations and their allied analysts, scholars, and researchers have worked to promote a perception of the "rules of the game" that limits the discussion of corporate practice (and the criticism thereof) to a relatively narrow field of acceptable issues. Following this analytical perspective, we would say that corporations' representatives have been active in seeking to define the new millennium's global political economy in ways that follow the interests of a specific (corporate) form of practice. This is far from uncontested and the success of such a venture varies from sector to sector of the global economy.

Fuchs develops this argument by suggesting that the power of corporations in global governance can be disaggregated into: instrumental power (direct means of influence); structural power, revolving around rule-making which can be rather more indirect, as the rules concerned require legislation and thus corporate influence is often linked primarily to national jurisdictions (or national diplomatic and negotiating teams in the international arena); and discursive power, linked to the manner in which certain settlements are politically legitimated outside the formal processes of policy adoption.[34] We can relatively easily identify the extent of direct/instrumental power of corporations (their economic "weight" as it were, with the provisos in place about size mentioned earlier), but it is the discursive, legitimating element that underpins the indirect influence, although this is much harder to easily identify in the global realm. Fuchs notes that one of the reasons that corporations have managed to expand their influence over debates concerned with the forms of political economic relations and global governance is that the policy discourse now encompasses a clear narrative of competitiveness, economic growth, and efficiency, all aspects of social practice that corporations have claimed as reflecting their own particular competences and skills.[35] It is unlikely that these developments have been accidental or organic, but rather can be directly related to a relatively explicit campaign by corporations and analysts to normalize their positive and constructive role in the growth and development of the global economy.

Surveying these "private sector entrepreneurs of regulatory change," Walter Mattli and Ngaire Woods have identified four broad incentives that encourage corporations to seek to influence and affect change in global governance (complementing the reasons why corporations are exposed to the regulatory practices of the WTO). Firstly, corporations that rely on the services of other market actors may seek to control or regulate their suppliers' economic power over them; for instance purchasing corporations may argue for de-regulation of price controls to promote competition and drive down their input costs. Secondly, new entrants to a specific economic sector may seek to remove or reduce barriers to entry through an engagement with the governing regime for that sector. Thirdly, and conversely, in both the above areas there are also corporations whose business model may be put at risk by such interventions; more generally corporations may seek regulatory change and innovation to limit the disruption caused by external developments (ranging from technical shifts to changing political exposure). Finally, seeing how the political tide is running, some corporations may seek to establish a "level playing field" for regulation, allowing them to consolidate their established position, and again potentially raising barriers to market entry for potential competitors, through arguments about "required" standards.[36] The key point, again, is there is not one driver behind corporate involvement with and engagement in global governance. We will return to the issue of how corporations develop and exercise their power and influence in much more detail in Chapter 4, but here I want to stress the multi-dimensionality of corporate power in global governance as a precursor to briefly mapping the terrain over which its exercise might be detected.

If global corporate power is multi-dimensional, varies by sector, and can be driven by differing corporate priorities it is unsurprising that sometimes corporations can be relatively ambivalent about engaging with international regulatory organizations at all. It is far from clear, for instance, that there was significant interest or engagement with the WTO's (failing) Doha round of multilateral trade negotiations, that sought to further remove and reduce impediments to free trade, in anything other than highly specialized areas (such as intellectual property rights—IPRs).[37] Rather corporations seem to have either acted through their home states, or taken little interest at all in contributing to the talks directly, where such opportunities may have arisen. Conversely, as has been well documented in the Uruguay Round of negotiations (that led to the formation of the WTO), a significant if small group of corporations played a major role in developing and shaping the TRIPs agreement to the extent that much of the drafting of the agreement was actually undertaken by legal teams either directly associated with specific corporations or employed by an association set up with the purpose of strengthening the protection of IPRs in the global system.[38] Likewise, the US-based Coalition of Service Industries (CSI) both worked to include services in the WTO's remit via the GATS, but has subsequently lobbied to expand and consolidate the range of services that states have opted-into as part of the variable aspect of the agreement. Moreover, the CSI has also been instrumental in establishing allied associations for service sector corporations in Europe and elsewhere, allowing its agenda to be progressed across the WTO membership,[39] in one of the few areas where developed state-based corporations still maintain some clear competitive advantage over competitors from emerging and developing economies. However, it is not the case that all such attempts to shape the legal structures of global governance are as direct, or as successful as this case.

The corporate involvement in and influence over the earlier Uruguay Round negotiations may have been exceptional rather than the establishment of a settled level of influence. A specific conjunction of circumstances, including the domination of the United States immediately after the end of the Cold War, the close cooperation between the European Union and US negotiators around an agenda that presented previous rounds of international trade negotiations (under the General Agreement on Tariffs and Trade—GATT) as having done too little to protect the market position of US and EU based corporations, and the (then) under-developed economic challenge of the emerging and developing states.[40] This shift to a more accommodating stance as regards corporate interests has been further facilitated by the close relationship between the International Chamber of Commerce and the WTO secretariat, including regular staff movements between the organizations. This increased engagement with the global corporate sector has also partly been the driver to more civil society engagement with the WTO, not least of all as the WTO's establishing agreement encourages a wider range of stakeholder involvement than for the treaty arrangements which are replaced.[41] Thus, while critics bemoan the involvement of corporations in the negotiations and everyday workings of the WTO, this has actually been (perhaps not fully) balanced by a much more open approach to international trade negotiations and regulation than had previously been evident.

Seeing the latest (Doha) Round of negotiations as focusing on little that is to their direct advantage, having "locked in" many of their key demands through the WTO's established set of rules (settled in the Uruguay Round), corporations have now often moved their attention from the trade negotiations to the WTO's dispute settlement mechanism (DSM). Reflecting the range of interests set out above, developing state based corporations have often sought in the last decade to use the DSM to work to open markets where their international cost advantages are significant; here the role of Brazil's trade team (assisted by academics and trade associations) is exemplary of the manner by which the corporate interest can be furthered at the WTO. The Brazilian team seems to have identified markets where their national corporations would be able to compete successfully and then sought to ensure full WTO-compliant access has been achieved sometimes in the face of non-formalized modes of "protection."[42] As this suggests it is also not the case that all corporations share the same interests; often developing and emerging economy based corporations seek to open mature developed state markets that developed country corporations would rather see more heavily regulated (to ensure high barriers to market entry). Indeed, it is more accurate to see the institutions of global governance as a terrain over which inter-corporate rivalry and competition takes place, rather than merely the subject of one-dimensional corporate influence.

Nevertheless, corporations also often work together where clear general and/or sectoral interests might be best articulated and prosecuted through a range of collective organizations from focused lobbying groups to general (business) interest associations. For instance, the European Round Table of Industrialists founded in 1983 represents

European corporations—members include the chairs or chief executive officers of Beyer, Fiat, BP, Shell, Unilever, Siemens and Renault—reinforcing personal networks through its institutionalization into various economic/commercial focused EU committees.[43] Likewise corporate leaders, analysts and politicians meet at events such as the annual World Economic Forum (WEF) in Davos, where interactions, private lobbying, and influence can have often quite significant long-term impact on the forms of corporate interaction with states and other governance mechanisms, and how the broad corporate interest is articulated in policy discourses.

Alongside the WEF, other organizations including the Trilateral Commission, the World Business Council for Sustainable Development and Trans-Atlantic Business Dialogue are all forums where senior corporate managers (and shareholders) can work to influence and shape state activities as regards the global governance of the corporate sector. These and other organizations are closely linked with highly centralized networks and an inner circle represented by the largest global corporations able to articulate a clear global business interest as regards the regulation of the global market system.[44] Again, sometimes the interest represented by these groups generally reflects the views of the global corporate sector overall, while in other cases the interests being expressed will be related to specific sectors or regions and only reflect the perspective of some corporations. Whatever the position being developed, while not a (directly effective) governance mechanism in itself, these various (and often changing) networks are often able to shape and influence the agenda of the global governance with some alacrity; we will return to these issues in Chapter 4.

Global corporations as institutions of global governance themselves

In addition to being affected by and seeking to influence institutions of global governance, a number of corporate actors also effectively act as global governance institutions in themselves, wielding influence over the global system in one way or another. These corporations and (profit-making) associations may gather power and governance functions to themselves through states' recognition of their expertise and technical knowledge resources, or through the successful independent assertion of such expertise. This dovetails to a large extent with the elements of private authority in the global system that have been subject to considerable interest by a range of political economists in the last quarter century,[45] although the organizations that I briefly focus on here are profit-focused corporations rather than private associations of other kinds. Organizations focused on regulating a specific issue and the corporations involved often come together in multi-stakeholder initiatives which include the setting of standards and goals, alongside some framework for collective decision-making and forms of promoting and achieving the proposed standards, such as certification schemes (potentially policed though consumer choice).[46] However, in some arenas particular corporations may be able to carve out significant regulatory power without necessarily directly or extensively engaging stakeholders; here corporations that successfully promote proprietary technical standards have the ability to shape (and thus govern) practice in certain arenas. Technology standards (including the network effects of wide adoption) are perhaps the most obvious example, typified by what (when it was most ascendant and evident) was referred to as Wintelism (the force of IBM and Microsoft's ability to shape the global development of personal computing),[47] although interestingly this is now in relatively rapid decline in the face of new mobile computing technologies (with Apple and Google in the vanguard).

Perhaps the most obvious non-technology organizations that fall into this category are the international credit ratings agencies of which the two best known are Moody's and Standard & Poor, both based in the United States. These agencies rate the credit worthiness of bonds and other financial instruments (debt) and their judgments have become the stuff of daily news media business reporting. Like the IASB their power has been strengthened where their standards have been adopted by states and international organizations, such as when state laws require pension funds' various holdings not to drop below a certain level of credit worthiness as measured by one or other of these agencies. Their power has been enhanced by the increased global mobility of capital and thus the need for non-nationals to have some way of quickly judging the risk of various potential investments.[48] However, their role in global governance (as a private authority) is also partly constrained by the (mostly) voluntary character of the ratings offered (indeed those being rated are charged, leading to claims of a conflict of interest in the rating process), and the choice among a second tier of (sometimes national) ratings agencies which offer alternative ratings.

To some extent given their authority to judge whether corporations are reporting their financial affairs correctly (in line with the IFRS), the large international accountancy companies also have a regulatory or governance role. However, and like the credit ratings agencies, this ability is weakened by the ability of corporation to choose other (perhaps only nationally operating) companies to audit their accounts, even if this may have some reputational impact. Equally as their judgments are provisional, with the final arbiter of financial reporting remaining state institutions, this role while playing a part in the general governance regime for corporations remains complementary to it rather than completely and independently regulatory. Moreover, the ability of the "big four" accountancy firms to mobilize a shift in the agenda of regulation has been partially tainted by accountancy scandals, like that which brought down Arthur Andersen (in this case linked to the demise of Enron). Despite their clear regulatory role (shaping and limiting the flow of investment funds for instance), unlike other elements of global governance these actors are not (even in the final analysis) accountable to states or other well-established legitimate authorities (such as the UN).

Finally as will be developed in the chapter on corporate governance the global corporation itself has a significant governance role within its own international structures. The extended and complex supply chains utilized by many corporations, bringing together a wide and varied group of subsidiaries, associated and independent suppliers requires significant levels of governance to maintain the flow of products (and services) for the core corporation. Highly developed internal networks of control and cross-ownership are required reflecting a governance function that while largely limited to their own network(s), by virtue of the global reach of such networks parallels many of the issues that are more traditionally identified as of importance to the realm of global governance dominated by international government organizations.

Conclusion

This chapter has sought to set out the range of issues which the rest of the book will deal with in some more detail. The key point has been to stress that global corporations feel the effects of global governance in various ways (and to various degrees) and as such, given their developed diplomatic function, we should be unsurprised that they seek to influence and shape the modes of governance they confront in their everyday activities. Moreover it is mistaken to assume that corporations are always external actors in the realm of global governance; rather at different times and for different issues they are both inside global governance looking out, and outside looking in.

Reflecting on corporations' interactions with global governance, some commentators for instance would argue that the lack of a major shift in state environmental policies, despite the negotiation of the

Kyoto Protocol can be linked to the ability of corporations to present their general requirement for relatively light environmental regulation as underpinning continued growth and economic prosperity; by framing policy choices in this manner, corporate lobbyists have ensured that Kyoto and other environmental initiatives are weaker instruments than many of their most vocal promoters had hoped.[49] Conversely some corporations have promoted (and regulated) sustainable practices within their own supply chains and networks while maintaining that this is best achieved via guidelines and not formalized regulation. The key question often posed is whether this political influence over the forms of environmental response is legitimate or anti-democratic. It is worth me being explicit at this point: the position that I develop in the rest of the book does not seek to demonize global corporations as always exercising illegitimate influence or conversely to defend them against their critics, but rather seeks to explore their interaction with global governance institutions on the grounds that this has been an under-recognized aspect of the mainstream analysis of global governance. Certainly, there are cases where one might suggest that the influence and power of global corporations has been problematic or illegitimate, but equally there are often good reasons for corporate interest in global governance practices and perfectly legitimate expectations that their voice should be heard in the deliberations over developments in globalized regulation and governance, not least of all as these practices may be internal to their working practices and networks. One key criticism of the corporate interest has been the question of whether their political-legal character itself indicates that their role in governance almost by definition is a challenge to accepted and legitimate processes of (global) governance. It is to that political-legal character that we turn in the next chapter.

Notes

1 Craig Murphy, *International Organization and Industrial Change: Global Governance Since 1850* (London: Polity Press, 1994).
2 See: Stephen Wrage and Alexandra Wrage, "Multinational Enterprises as 'Moral Entrepreneurs' in a Global Prohibition Regime Against Corruption," *International Studies Perspectives* 6 (2005): 316–324; or Hans Krause Hansen, "Governing Corruption through the Global Corporation" in *Business and Global Governance*, ed. M. Ougaard and A. Leander (London: Routledge, 2010): 118–137.
3 See: Mathias Koenig-Archibugi, "Transnational Corporations and Public Accountability," *Government and Opposition* 39, No. 2 (Spring 2004): 234–259; or Ronald W. Cox, ed., *Corporate Power and Globalization in US Foreign Policy* (London: Routledge, 2012).

4 Doris Fuchs, *Business Power in Global Governance* (Boulder, Colo.: Lynne Rienner Publishers, 2007), 94.

5 John Stopford and Susan Strange, *Rival States, Rival Firms: Competition for World Market Shares* (Cambridge: Cambridge University Press, 1991).

6 John Stopford, "Revisiting Rival States: Beyond the Triangle?" in *International Business and Government Relations in the 21st Century*, ed. R. Grosse (Cambridge: Cambridge University Press, 2005), 103–115.

7 Merja Pentikäinen, "Changing International 'Subjectivity' and Rights and Obligations under International Law – Status of Corporations" *Utrecht Law Review* 8, No. 1 (January 2012): 145–154.

8 Virginia Haufler, "Global Governance and the Private Sector" in *Global Corporate Power* (IPE Yearbook 15) ed. C. May (Boulder, Colo.: Lynne Rienner, 2006), 91.

9 Donna E. Arzt, and Igor I Lukashuk, "Participants in International Legal Relations" in *Beyond Confrontation: International Law for the Post-Cold War Era*, ed. L.F. Damrosch, G. Danielenkdo, and R. Mullerson (Washington, DC: American Society of International Law, 1995) [reprinted in *International Law: Classic and Contemporary Readings* (second edition), eds C. Ku and P.F. Diehl (Boulder, Colo.: Lynne Rienner, 2003), 45–62].

10 Sarianna M. Lundan, "Regulating Global Corporate Capitalism" in *The Handbook of Global Companies*, ed. J. Mikler (Chichester: John Wiley & Sons, 2013), 247.

11 Peter T. Muchlinski, *Multilateral Enterprises and the Law* (second edition), (Oxford: Oxford University Press, 2007), Chapter 15.

12 Haufler, "Global Governance and the Private Sector"; Peter Utting, "Introduction: Multistakeholder regulation from a development perspective" in *Business Regulation and Non-State Actors: Whose standards? Whose development?*, ed. D. Reed, P. Utting, and A. Mukherjee-Reed (London: Routledge, 2012), 1–17.

13 Rainer Lanz, and Sébastien Miroudot, *Intra-Firm Trade: Patterns, Determinants and Policy Implications* (OECD Trade Policy Papers No. 114) (Paris: OECD Publishing, 2011).

14 This list adapted and amended from: Thomas Brewer and Stephen Young, "Multilateral Institutions and Policies: Implications for Multinational Business Strategy" in *The Oxford Handbook of International Business*, ed. A. Rugman (Oxford: Oxford University Press, 2009), 291, and *passim*.

15 Steve McGuire, "What Happened to the Influence of Business? Corporations and Organized Labor at the WTO" in *The Oxford Handbook on the World Trade Organization*, ed. A. Narlikar, M. Daunton, and R.M. Stern (Oxford: Oxford University Press, 2012), 329.

16 Alan O. Sykes, "The Dispute Settlement Mechanism: Ensuring Compliance" in *The Oxford Handbook on the World Trade Organization*, ed. A. Narlikar, M. Daunton, and R.M. Stern (Oxford: Oxford University Press, 2012), 567.

17 James Perry and Andreas Nölke, "The Political Economy of International Accounting Standards" *Review of International Political Economy* 13, no. 4 (October 2006): 559–586. At the time of writing (Summer 2014), after 12 years of negotiations, joint guidelines had just been published to bring together aspects of revenue reporting in the USA and in the rest of the world; while still not a comprehensive settlement to standardize reporting

protocols, the draft agreement covers the reporting of revenue for contracts with customers that in recent years has prompted some (acquisition related) controversies about advance booking of projected income.

18 John Braithwaite and Peter Drahos, *Global Business Regulation* (Cambridge: Cambridge University Press, 2000), Chapter 19.
19 The guidelines are available at http://www.oecd.org/daf/inv/mne/48004323.pdf.
20 Lundan, "Regulating Global Corporate Capitalism," 247–248.
21 Georg Kell and John Ruggie, "Global Markets and Social Legitimacy: The Case of the 'Global Compact'" in *The Market or the Public Domain: Global Governance and the Asymmetry of Power*, ed. D. Drache (London: Routledge, 2001), 323.
22 John Gerard Ruggie, "Taking Embedded Liberalism Global: The Corporate Connection" in *Taming Globalization: Frontiers of Governance*, ed. D. Held and M. Koenig-Archibugi (Cambridge: Polity Press, 2003), 113.
23 Ibid., 113.
24 Jem Bendell, *Flags of Inconvenience? The Global Compact and the Future of the United Nations* (International Centre for Corporate Social Responsibility: Research paper No. 22–2004) (Nottingham: ICCSR/Nottingham University Business School, 2004), 17.
25 Anne-Marie Slaughter, "Sovereignty and Power in a Networked World Order" *Stanford Journal of International Law* 40, no. 2 (2004), 310.
26 Kell and Ruggie, "Global Markets and Social Legitimacy," 330.
27 Bendall, *Flags of Inconvenience?*; Catia Gregoratti, "The United Nations Global Compact and development" in *Business Regulation and Non-State Actors: Whose standards? Whose development?*, ed. D. Reed, P. Utting, and A. Mukherjee-Reed (London: Routledge, 2012): 95–108.
28 David Vogel, "The Private Regulation of Global Corporate Conduct: Achievements and Limitations," *Business and Society* 49, no. 1 (2010): 68–87.
29 David Vogel, "The Private Regulation of Global Corporate Conduct" in *The Politics of Global Regulation*, ed. W. Mattli and N. Woods (Princeton, N.J.: Princeton University Press, 2009), 172.
30 Ibid., 176–177.
31 Vogel, "The Private Regulation of Global Corporate Conduct: Achievements and Limitations," 82
32 *The Economist*, "Schumpeter: The butterfly effect," 2 November 2013, 71.
33 Fuchs, *Business Power in Global Governance*.
34 Ibid., 66.
35 Ibid., 153.
36 Walter Mattli and Ngaire Woods, "In Whose Benefit? Explaining Regulatory Change in Global Politics" in *The Politics of Global Regulation*, ed. W. Mattli and N. Woods (Princeton, N.J.: Princeton University Press, 2009), 32–36.
37 McGuire, "What Happened to the Influence of Business?," 331.
38 Christopher May and Susan Sell, *Intellectual Property Rights: A Critical History* (Boulder, Colo.: Lynne Rienner, 2005), Chapter 7.
39 Sharon Beder, "Business-managed Democracy: The Trade Agenda," *Critical Social Policy* 30, no. 4 (2010), 506–507.
40 McGuire, "What Happened to the Influence of Business?," 328.
41 Cornelia Woll, "Global Companies as Agenda Setters in the World Trade Organization" in *The Handbook of Global Companies*, ed. J. Mikler (Chichester: John Wiley & Sons, 2013), 264–266.

42 McGuire, "What Happened to the Influence of Business?," 332–333.

43 Beder, "Business-managed democracy," 502.

44 William K. Carroll and Jean Phillipe Sapinski, "The Global Corporate Elite and the Transnational Policy-Planning Network 1996–2006: A Structural Analysis," *International Sociology* 25, no. 4 (2010): 501–538.

45 For instance: Rodney Bruce Hall and Thomas J. Biersteker, eds. *The Emergence of Private Authority in Global Governance* (Cambridge: Cambridge University Press, 2002).

46 Haufler, "Global Governance and the Private Sector," 96.

47 Michael Borrus and John Zysman, "Globalization with Borders: The Rise of Wintelism as the Future of Global Competition," *Industry and Innovation* 4, no. 2 (1997): 141–166.

48 Timothy J. Sinclair, *The New Masters of Capital: American Bond Rating Agencies and the Politics of Creditworthiness* (Ithaca, NY: Cornell University Press, 2005).

49 Robert Falkner, "Business and Global Climate Governance: A Neo-pluralist Perspective" in *Business and Global Governance*, ed. M. Ougaard and A. Leander (London: Routledge, 2010): 99–117.

2 The legal personality of the corporation

Having set out the general set of issues we will be examining in this book, I shall now look at the key question of how the corporation can be conceived as a legal person (with attendant political economic rights). This issue has concerned a number of critics of the corporation; for instance, Laurence Boulle cautions that:

> [t]he rise of [multinational corporations] has further weakened the concept of citizenship for individuals, and in a certain sense [multinational corporations] themselves have replaced natural persons as the 'citizens' of economic globalization … In reality, globalization has elevated the freedom to trade and other market-related liberties to a higher order than the various civil and political freedoms associated with individuals and social groups. Moreover the corporation and not the individual is a major direct beneficiary of the freedom to trade.[1]

Therefore, it makes sense to examine the extension of "citizenship" rights to corporations, and ask what it is about the corporation that makes such an entitlement plausible. The discussion of citizenship has two clear dimensions: firstly, the ability of the corporation, identified as a legal person, to enjoy the established rights of citizens within political systems; this is the subject of this chapter. Secondly, there is the aspiration to "good citizenship" by corporations, often linked to corporate social responsibility. Here "citizenship" is seen as an indicator of moral standing, with supporters of corporate social responsibility presenting corporate (good) citizenship as a positive move towards ethical political economy; this is taken up in the next chapter.

First, it is worth noting that there is one major and abiding difference between natural persons and corporate persons; while we can recognize that a human being is a person without aid of the law (even if the law accords some clear rights and responsibilities to that recognition), the corporate person is entirely dependent on the law for this status. Legal personality is inter-subjective, inasmuch as the legal person(s) can only act on this basis when recognized by others of a similar standing (and thereby establish a legal relation), but for the natural person a relationship can be established with others outside any legal recognition of personhood;[2] humanity, and the recognition of persons as similar (what we might refer to as empathy) precedes the law. The corporation can only enjoy personhood because the law allows it; the natural person enjoys personhood by being a human being. However, it is also the case that many things that persons can do (as economic actors), such as hold property and dispose of (sell) it, or contract with others, are only possible when the person is recognized as so enabled in law. At various times natural persons have been excluded from such rights to act in states and jurisdictions that have limited the rights of certain groups—apartheid being an obvious example—and many societies still limit rights on the basis of age, and/or on the basis of gender.[3] Natural persons and corporate persons therefore can be distinguished clearly in certain ways but significant commonalities can also be identified, and it is this that we will focus on below.

The shape of corporate legal personality

Although corporations are organizations made up of groups of people, encompassing various social and internal institutions, with capital (and other) assets mobilized towards a set of economic (and sometimes extra-economic) ends, they are usually treated also as having a single personality for legal purposes. This is particularly beneficial in contract law: the corporation can be dealt with as a single signatory to agreements and undertakings, much as a natural person might; this makes negotiations clear and ensures that responsibility for fulfillment of a contract's provisions is allocated effectively. The legal personality of the corporation also has a distinct political dimension that needs to be considered in assessing the relationship between corporations and global governance. This legal form arguably was subject to some democratic deliberation in the United Kingdom and the United States during its development in the nineteenth and twentieth centuries, but as it has been adopted (to various degrees) across the global system, there has been less chance for local political groups (or a nascent global civil society) to have any significant impact on its character. As I noted in the introduction, there are other modes of corporate organization, but the Anglo-Saxon legal form is both influential and widespread, not least because of preferences around stock market listing(s), and it is therefore mainly this form of corporate personhood on which I will focus, accepting that it is not universal and not without internal variations.

The general dimensions and legal characteristics of the contemporary corporation, as Phillip Blumberg has pointed out, involve the "recognition of particular rights and responsibilities—one by one—that shape the juridical contours of the legal unit for which they have been created."[4] These characteristics have been established and molded by law: through statutory regulation; through judicial precedent (in common law systems); and via emerging models of international "soft law" regulation. The core set of rights that are generally recognized in most developed country jurisdictions, and elsewhere, are:

- the right to a name (and thus to have an identity);
- the right to sue and be sued;
- the right to acquire, hold and dispose of property;
- the right to contract; and
- specified rights under various constitutional and legislative provisions.

[and specifically as regards corporations]

- continued existence, notwithstanding a change in membership or share ownership;
- limited liability of members for organizational legal responsibility; and
- central direction of management.[5]

While there are also some possible responsibilities attached to a corporation's activity, these are generally somewhat circumscribed by the impact of limited liability, and the frequent difficulty of establishing the location of decisions that might have led to offences that could require sanction under law.[6] For instance, in the United Kingdom the difficulty of establishing a single "directing mind" has undermined past attempts to prosecute corporate manslaughter, despite its statutory introduction as a crime.

The legal personality of the corporation might also be seen as an aspect of the structural power of business. By some accounts it excessively empowers business and constrains policy options in a way that can be detrimental to democracy; these "persons" can wield influence in a manner seldom possible for natural persons by virtue of the resources they control and direct.[7] However, discussions of democracy often take the corporate form as so self-evidently a standard functional feature of society that it is not worthy of comment, or even necessarily noticed; as such this normalizing or naturalizing of a social fact might be one indication of the influence of forms of agenda-setting or corporate structural power. Indeed, legislative changes to the corporate form are often presented as relatively minor adjustments and almost exclusively involve corporate lawyers, courts, and specialized legislative committees, with little or no involvement of the general public. Nevertheless, the establishment of the common-sense of corporate personhood requires us to examine its elements and explore the claimed parallels with the rights and responsibilities of natural persons in political society.

Starting with early company law, the corporation was regarded as being formed for a specified purpose and thus subject to the legal principle of *ultra vires*: that it could only lawfully do what it had been set up to (alongside the contributory actions that might be implied by such an undertaking).[8] Again, at least initially this was another distinction between natural persons and corporate persons (under common law systems at least) in that natural persons could (and still can) legally do anything not specifically prohibited by the law, while corporations could only do that which was part of their legally defined activity. Nowadays this distinction has largely faded, although governments still remain governed by the principle. Other distinctions between natural and corporate persons have also been dissolved either through shifts in customary practice or the direct involvement of judicial authorities. For instance, in one recent development, in the United States in 2010, the (notorious) *Citizens United* judgment by the US Supreme Court, extended the fourteenth amendment's protection of free speech to corporations, and specifically allowed an unfettered right to *political* speech—which is to say, in this case, to undertake political advertising campaigns.[9] Here, the difference between the rights available to a corporate person and natural persons have been brought into alignment by a positive extension of the rights of the corporate person where such rights in the past had been specifically regarded as inappropriate given the extensive resources that corporations can apply to their freedom of (political) speech.

For natural persons, citizenship is directly tied to the state (and its jurisdiction), but where globally focused corporations have moved away from a tight connection to their originating state/domicile, a more complex citizenship has been developed: corporations may identify with their "home" state for political bargaining purposes, but they often are also seeking to present themselves as citizens of a global economy to investors, *denationalizing* their character to maximize the potential to gain investment funds and expand economic relations beyond the immediate allies of their home state.[10] In national and global politics, the engagement of corporations can be positive, negative, or even both, depending on the political views of the commentator and also the scope or purpose of the engagement itself. Nevertheless, in all cases it is the corporation as single political and legal person who is regarded as the political actor concerned.

The corporation is, however, not merely perceived as a single political actor from the outside; the rights of legal personhood also allow the corporation to clearly control its various assets (human, infrastructural, and intangible) and deploy them to a set of defined ends (most usually set by the management of the corporation), by establishing a single and definable locus of authority. This localized (within the corporation itself) political power is constituted by the state through the legal arrangements put in place via the law for incorporation, and the associated legal structures of company law, employment law, and other salient regulatory apparatus. Of these, perhaps the most important is the law of limited liability for the shareholders of the corporation.

Limited liability and the absent owner

As noted earlier, the shareholders of corporations are able to limit their liability to claims that stem from the activities of the corporation itself, or the consequences of those actions, ranging from debt to damages. This arrangement is hardly a direct analogue to the plight of the natural person, who is usually held responsible for the consequences of their actions, although equally there is no division between the natural person and their (self) ownership that compares with shareholding. At its most basic the justification for limited liability is that it allows accelerated economic development and activity as those undertaking investment in such work are able to limit their exposure to risk to the original amount they felt able to stake or invest; there are no further calls on their assets other than those which they have voluntarily undertaken. However, it is sometimes forgotten that the legal personality of the corporation also extends this protection in the other direction as well. The assets of the corporation are protected from the creditors of the shareholders of the corporation; the distancing that law achieves is symmetrical, insulating the corporate economy from the personal economy of its owners.

Many of the claimed advantages of limited liability and joint stock endeavors came into clear focus during the acceleration of economic activity around the industrial revolution. By the mid-nineteenth century the vast infrastructure projects that would establish the railways as a transformative technology required not merely bringing together large numbers of investors into risky projects, they also required centralized direction and coordination; the joint stock company with a single management structure was an effective solution to the organization of such projects if they were not to be public works. However, the reception of proposals to establish limited liability had not been uncontested, with earlier criticism focused on the impunity from the consequences of collective decisions and the absence of a single accountable person. Financial scandals (such as the South Sea Bubble) had slowed the development of the joint-stock company and made limited liability politically and socially suspect, but its legal form gained renewed traction in the later eighteenth century through the large number of Canal Acts that set up infrastructure (joint-stock) companies to develop that century's key infrastructure.[11] The success of these projects and the perceived need to build another new infrastructure (railways) for industrialized capitalism won out, and by the mid-nineteenth century the joint stock corporation extending limited liability to its investors was normalized as a general model, without the requirement of individual acts of parliament to establish it.[12] Not for the last time the "logic" of economic development was deployed to suggest that the transformation of the legal structure of the corporation served the well-established socio-economic ends of progress and growth.

Moreover, foreshadowing the privatization cycle of the late twentieth century, after an initial period of suspicion and some well-known failures, in the late nineteenth century the floating of successful consumer companies (perhaps most importantly Guinness and the sewing cotton suppliers J&P Coats) galvanized stock broking and accelerated it along the road towards its role in the economy 100 years later.[13] Stock and shares became (and continue to be) an acceptable and socially significant asset class for investors, from professionals to amateurs seeking to invest small amounts of savings. This led to the increasing division between ownership and control of the corporation, with Thorstein Veblen suggesting in the early twentieth century that the absentee owner (in a direct parallel to the absentee landlord) was emblematic of an impersonal and irresponsible capitalism, with few moral links between the rights of ownership (shares) and the consequences of corporate actions.[14] The fragmented ownership structure of the modern corporation allowed the owners to sidestep responsibility for the practices undertaken in their interest. However, equally the shielding of owners from responsibility (it is often claimed) is what allows shares to be traded easily and for pools of investors' capital to be mobilized effectively to support the development and continuance of the economic activity required for social wellbeing, about which the investors themselves require little specialized or technical knowledge.

One "solution" to the problem the (ir)responsibility of owners (of shares) has been the recent closer tying of shareholders to management, not least through share-based incentive and reward schemes that have sought to align owners and managers and re-introduce owners' control and thereby responsibility for the actions of the corporation. Unfortunately, as limited liability remains entrenched, all this has done is expand those who benefit from the positive rewards for (sometimes extreme) risk taking by the corporation, while continuing to limit the costs of failure.[15] Conversely, as Paddy Ireland suggests, a different solution to the problem of "irresponsibility" would be to separate the rights to income and property (the share) from the rights to control; here the corporation's management would have the right to control the corporation as they saw fit (and associated responsibility for actions) severed from shareholder "interference."[16] Interestingly for David Ciepley, this is exactly the situation that already exists:

> The shareholders are not management's authorizing principal. In the eyes of corporate law, the principal is the corporation itself, and management its agent. Management has a duty to act on behalf of the corporation (and not simply on behalf of its shareholders), and in discharging this duty, is authorized to rule over corporate personnel and property. Both this duty and this authorization come from the state, via a corporate charter.[17]

Incorporation therefore separates the shareholders *qua* owners from the actual ownership of corporations' assets (formally owned by the corporation itself), requires managers to comply not only with general legal principles but also with the specifics of corporate law, and crucially reveals the state to be the foundation of the corporation's particular political economy by virtue of the corporation's reliance on legal structures for its form and practice. The managers of corporations are likely to be influenced more by the legal context in which the corporation operates than by the wishes of the shareholders, other than in an abstract sense that the corporation is required to focus on "shareholder value" (as we will discuss later).

Finally, while debates continue about the ability to hold corporations morally responsible for their actions, reflected in the development of corporate social responsibility, shareholders have remained shielded from such concerns (other than how such ascription of responsibility impacts on share-price, which it seems seldom to do). Given the wide recognition of the moral responsibility of individuals and the role of such natural persons in the management of corporations, ascribing some moral responsibility to corporations and indeed to their managers and employees should hardly be controversial even if the justifications for such ascription remain subject to some discussion.[18] However, the reach of morality into corporate affairs usually stops well short of ascribing any moral responsibility to the owners of shares, with the limitation of liability usually seen as an established and normal social fact.

The political economy of corporate personhood

As I have already mentioned, a common approach to the corporation's organizational character sees the establishment of a single organizational identity as a clear benefit to economic efficiency. Rather than having to develop a network of contracted inter-relations, the corporate form (as a single entity) facilitates the development of a hierarchy within which economic activity can be arranged and directed, and also regulated by external actors/agencies. Thus, a corporation as contracting "person" can employ natural persons without necessarily explicitly describing their task; rather the authority structured through a hierarchical relationship allows both flexibility and agility *within* its economic activities (it is a form of self-contained political realm). However, the internal relations of the corporation *qua* person are governed by law unlike the internal (or close) social relations of natural persons that are subject to more normative shaping (for instance in familial relations) albeit with legal limitations on behavior (such as those around child abuse). This has led David Ciepley to regard the corporation as constitutional republic, enjoying many governmental-like powers within its own organization, although the employees of a shareholder republic enjoy few if any of the democratic rights (other than those imposed by law) enjoyed by citizens of state-republics.[19] These arrangements are justified by the economic (and therefore social welfare) benefits that organizing activity in this manner can produce. As we will see this can also be identified at the global level by virtue of a (global) corporation's global-governance-like role within its own complex networks and relations.

The danger is that an account of the corporate form, centered on the development of limited liability might be regarded as being overly functional or allowing too much weight to its economic determinants. As Paddy Ireland has pointed out:

> One of the effects of the dominance of the economically determinist account, in which corporate law is seen as a simple expression of economic and technological imperatives, is the naturalization and de-politicization of the corporate form and its key constituent elements: separate corporate personality, limited liability, shareholder primacy and so on. They are, in effect, placed beyond critical examination and evaluation, and a case is implicitly made for their global extension.[20]

This suggestion has prompted Gary Wilson to re-examine the history of corporate personality through an analysis that builds on Karl Polanyi's concept of the double movement. In Polanyi's analysis the historical and progressive removal of markets from their social context (making them independent of much of the social and normative milieu of society) in the nineteenth century prompted a politico-social reaction to re-embed these transactions in the socially established normative realm through new government regulation and legal structures.[21] The key point that is relevant here is that the corporate form (whatever its economic advantages) is the result of state legal action (legislation). Once, in Polanyian terms, the corporate form had been used to disembed corporate affairs from the social milieu, locating them in an exclusively *economic* sphere, the politico-social dynamic Polanyi identified prompted political actors to seek to *re-embed* the corporate form into a socially responsive political economy.

As the perceived problems of corporate irresponsibility became clearer over the course of the twentieth century, so social forces of one sort or another sought to find ways to control and limit the freedoms that the initial legal practices of incorporation had achieved.[22] The notion of the corporation as legal person became the focus for innovations intended to modify (or even undo) some of the freedoms extended through incorporation. This has ranged from developments in the regulation of corporate affairs—including employment legislation, standard setting, and the regulation of products produced by corporations (food safety and content requirements, to automobile safety regulations)—to the emergence of private initiatives to set standards for corporate behavior, the latter often latterly gathered together under the rubric of corporate social responsibility or corporate citizenship (in the second sense alluded to at the start of this chapter). These developments are the subject of the next chapter, but, of course, are not the only aspects of the corporation's political economy to be subject to criticism.

Another serious political issue raised by corporate personality and limited liability is the ownership of shares in one corporation by another. Frequently, this is not merely a company in which a corporation seeks to invest; rather this is an important form of corporate network governance. External to the corporation, there may be subsidiaries and affiliates that it either wholly or partly owns, but as a share-holding legal person, the corporation is able to enjoy the rights of limited liability as regards these connected business units. The coming together of legal personality and limited liability allows a complex corporate network to have "firebreaks" or insulation to prevent risk and damages being transmitted back through the complex structure to the owning concern. When I return to the question of the global politics of corporate taxation, such ownership structures will be center-stage. Like so many questions that might be the focus of attention in (global) corporate affairs, the root of this issue is the issue of the acceptable level of equality in (legal) treatment between the corporate person and the natural person.

On the one hand, despite the relatively clear differences between natural and corporate persons, it may be the case that corporations should be considered to be "quasi citizens," in the first sense alluded to at the start of the chapter.[23] These quasi citizens both seek to protect themselves from the power of the state (invoking rights to operate, and protection from "unlawful" restrictions on their activities) while also working to lever state power for their own benefit (subsidies, tax holidays, and international protection for their property rights, and ability to enter new markets).[24] The corporation has the right to engage in political activities that are analogous to those of the natural person *qua* citizen, albeit subject to some constraints, to secure these protections and benefits. However, the benefits the corporate citizen derives from the state are not directly comparable with the benefits natural persons may receive, but indeed may often dwarf (by virtue of scale of activity) those available to recipients of other forms of (social) welfare.[25] Moreover, the forms of corporate welfare that are directly analogous to the welfare available to natural persons are often either hidden or obscured, but are nonetheless part of the political relationship between a corporate citizen and its (home) state.

To be clear, this is not to argue that unlike other citizens corporations do not have legitimate welfare needs and expectations vis-à-vis

the state, only that often this is not clearly set out, the costs and benefits transparently accounted for and scrutinized in the same terms as
social welfare (especially under "austerity") when it is natural persons
who are the recipients or beneficiaries. Thus, for instance, in the United
Kingdom income support from the state helps those whose weekly
income falls below a certain threshold for an acceptable income for
families. However, this can be regarded not (only) as a benefit to the
individual but also to the employer as it allows a lower wage to be paid,
and a higher level of profit to be maintained (by keeping wage costs
lower). This is seldom presented in the media as a benefit to employers,
however, even while other benefits to citizens become subject to arguments about welfare dependence and eligibility; it is seldom suggested
that these employers have become dependent on welfare to make a
profit. There is an asymmetry in the manner in which corporations'
and natural persons' citizenship right and responsibilities appear in
political debates.

The "problem" of the global corporate "person"

Although under various national jurisdictions there are relatively easily
identified common features that underpin a legal conception of the
corporation, this does not extend into the legal realm beyond the state.
Partly by virtue of the multi-faceted and often changeable ownership
and organizational structures of multinational corporations, there
remains no clear legal concept of the *multinational* corporation under
international law.[26] As corporate law has not been harmonized across
the global political economy, any internationalization of the legal form
that has taken place has been achieved either through (attempted)
extra-territorial jurisdiction or via organizational convergence driven
by the corporations' own interests. This is not to say potential loci for
a globalized commercial law do not exist; perhaps the most obvious
location for such a legal regime would be the World Trade Organization
(WTO).[27] Joseph Stiglitz has observed that bilateral investment treaties
(BITs) have also acted to expand particular understandings of the
character and rights of corporations which undermine the ability of
some national counterparties to regulate corporate activity in line with
domestic mores and democratically expressed demands, at the same
time of internationalizing some corporate (legal) form(s).[28]

Moreover the legal character of corporate rights (to property and
protection of investments from policy "changes") in BITs is very different to what might be regarded as a set of balancing responsibilities
which are only established through "soft law" and voluntary standards.

International arbitration linked to investment treaties has extended the rights of corporations against the host states in which they may be investing, while at the same time attempts to apply regulatory oversight to their behavior have largely been constrained and diverted.[29] For Joseph Stiglitz, an international commercial court which was constituted to adjudicate on the basis of the host country's laws (not those of the BITs) would alleviate the anti-democratic promotion of (non-domestic) corporate rights above those of the citizens of countries in which they operate.[30] However, as José Alvarez puts it:

> Once a corporation is accepted as a person, it is more likely that the due process (and possibly other guarantees) applied to other persons (as in human rights regimes) would be seen as relevant and applicable within the investment regime ... While we know that what natural persons should be entitled to expect in terms of 'full protection' from the state and what businesses should be entitled to expect differ in reality (and perhaps morally) such distinctions may vanish (as they did in *Citizens United*) as corporate and other persons are assimilated.[31]

Therefore in the absence of positive international commercial law, the global corporation remains largely subject to national laws (albeit modified by international legal undertakings, such as BITs and membership of the WTO), and the self-regulation of its global practices.

This position on the international legal standing of the corporation is not universally held, however; there is a clear divide between the accommodating position that US legal authorities have developed through the case law associated with the US Alien Tort Claims Act (ATCA), and a European position that suggests the absence of a positive law depiction of the corporation as international legal subject precludes its consideration as such. The judicial position often deployed in the United States is that as international law is silent on any specific distinction between natural and juridical individuals, what is prohibited in international law as regards other "persons" must also be forbidden to corporate associations *qua* persons.[32] For some European commentators this issue is (partly) resolved by including corporations (and for that matter, other non-state actors) as "participants" in international legal relations, allowing some distinction between corporations who require national legal recognition (incorporation or similar) to establish their status and natural persons, who under international law have some basic rights not linked to any nationality or residence requirement.[33] That said; in the main corporations lack any direct exposure to international law, although indirectly through their national incorporation, international law does have some application to corporations' practices.[34] The International Criminal Court's legal remit, for instance, is explicitly limited to "natural persons," thereby excluding corporations from its jurisdiction.[35] This means that any attempt to subject specific activities of corporations to legal action under international criminal law requires that an individual or group of individuals in the corporation be identified as having caused the activity to happen. This is often referred to as the search for a "directing mind" in the organization, which given the complexity of decision-making especially in global corporations, has limited the current reach of international criminal law into the global corporate sector.[36]

A further difficulty is that not all actors we might regard as being corporate for the purposes of political economic analysis are corporate in the legal sense that dominates the discussion of the corporation in the global system. In emerging markets and developing countries, there are still large numbers of family owned business groups. Partly to spread risk and partly reflecting the manner in which enterprises have often developed historically, away from the developed states' economies, family led business groups often control a range of businesses across a number of sectors (resembling conglomerates).[37] To some extent this is a strategy against political and social changes that may impact certain markets, but also may result from their origination in trading operations rather than production. Moreover, in contrast with the many developed economies, in the emerging and developing economies there are also many more state owned enterprises. Here China is perhaps the most significant example as regards the extent of the economic activity, although there remain significant state owned corporations even in Europe, in the energy and postal sectors for instance. Especially as regards state-owned enterprises the extension of (international) legal personhood may have anomalous legal effects, not least of all as often the rights of the individual so recognized are held *against* states, and as such it is difficult to see how this could be resolved for state-owned enterprises. Nevertheless, for my argument I will focus on the corporation and its personality (legal or otherwise).

With this focus in mind it is worth comparing the potential situation of the shareholder nationally and internationally. In the national arena limited liability has allowed shareholders, should they so wish, to ignore corporate behavior and practices, focusing merely on the "financials." Certainly, shareholders can be active should they so wish, and indeed some do take varying levels of direct and positive interest in the activities of those corporations in which they have invested.

However, in the international arena and where corporations have shareholdings in other companies, often subsidiaries or commercial network partners (either in the supply chain or as part of distribution networks, for instance), then it is more likely that these shareholders take a much closer interest in the practices, activities, and behaviors of the companies and/or corporations in which they have invested. Equally though, the enjoyment of limited liability may shield owning corporations from the responsibility for decision-making,[38] allowing them to cut affiliates loose more easily than if they were fully inte-grated divisions, allowing them similar levels of "irresponsibility" that are enjoyed by natural persons as shareholders. Where major global corporations are the main or only shareholder of network partners, the conventions around corporate personhood (developed in national con-texts) and their relation to investors do not sit well with the actual practices and character of the global corporate sector as the central justification around the pooling of disparate capital is largely absent. Once again the question of divergence and convergence of natural and corporate persons illuminates the difficulties in defining the character of the corporate person vis-à-vis natural (rights holding) persons.

Conclusion

In general the corporation can be understood in nominalistic terms, where the shareholders control the managers and require such man-agers to act in ways that accord with the shareholders' interests, or it can be understood in a "realistic" manner where the corporation is largely free to merely consider its own survival and growth without as keen a requirement around profitability.[39] In the former analysis, unlike other legally recognized persons the corporation does not primarily act as its own agent responding to an internalized morality; rather in the guise of the resurgence of the primacy of shareholder value, corpora-tions are driven to deliver value to shareholders whatever the other potential costs. Senior managers' and owners' interests may be aligned through share-related performance measures and managerial share-holdings, with the "owners" now expected only to judge investments on the basis of the (relatively short-term) financial performance of their shares.[40] The market for ownership and control of corporations (which is dominated by institutional investors) has narrowed the range of expectations from ownership. In this we might say that while enjoying many of the protections and rights afforded to individuals the cor-poration has managed to sidestep many of the (legal and moral) responsibilities we expect other (natural) individuals to recognize as (internally, morally) shaping their actions. The focus on shareholder value can diminish the scope of consequences that are considered by the corporation when assessing its practical and organizational options.

The reason the second analytical position is referred to as "realistic" is that when one is dealing with a corporation on an everyday basis, while one might recognize that there are shareholders, the corporation itself is the legal entity being engaged with; there is no need to consider who the shareholders are or what their interests might be. Rather, the corporation exists in market relationships as a rights holding, contracting partner with whom an economic transaction of some form is undertaken. This is how we *really* deal with corporations when we encounter them; it is a useful simplification of what would otherwise be a more complex set of relations with a set of owners with varying fractional interest in the commercial relations being undertaken on their behalf by the corporation itself. However, in the promotion of shareholder value as the main focus for performance management, the distinction between these two perspectives has been clouded: shareholder value is an imputed, rather than necessarily explicitly expressed demand with the maximization of share-price the usual proxy for shareholder interest. At the same time as managers themselves have become significant shareholders, the notion of a division between ownership and control has been undermined.

Returning to the point made at the beginning of this chapter, unlike natural persons, corporations only enjoy legal personhood at the pleasure of the state (through the process of incorporation). One way to reconcile the corporate form with liberal democracy is to return to its original logic; a grant of authority by the state to carry out certain public purposes. In the seventeenth century when this first became widely used, these public purposes were defined by the state with relatively little public participation, but nevertheless were framed as public interests ranked above rights to private enrichment. Since then democracy has grown in importance as a crucial element in legitimizing the authority of the state and in identifying and implementing the public interest. As importantly, while there may be clear common law rights that corporations can legitimately expect to be upheld (linked to contract and property law for instance) it makes less sense for them to be able to assert rights against the state or government. As Ciepley observes: "corporations, having been constituted by government and having received their rights from government, cannot turn around and claim constitutional rights against government, as if like the People, they pre-existed government and had reserved rights against it."[41] Or looking at it from the other direction: "since natural persons are not dependent on government for their existence they—and through them their businesses [partnerships or proprietorships] *can* claim to have rights prior to the government that may be held against it."[42] This is to say if we accept some notion of social contractual argument about democracy and government, by virtue of requiring the state to establish their existence, corporations cannot have been part of the conditional transfer of popular sovereignty to the Leviathan (the modern state), and thereby cannot have limited their exposure to the power *of* the state. Moreover, if justice (and the rule of law) is concerned with equality in law, then treating corporations as rights holding (legal) persons violates this principle by treating two types of persons who are substantively not similar (in anything other than imputed legal terms) as if *they were* equal.[43] Indeed an argument that they deserve equal treatment because of their legal similarity is circular as it is the law itself that has *made* them similar, and thus such similarity is not separate from the character of the law itself. This suggests that there must be some distinction between corporate persons and natural persons if the law and democratic political deliberation are to function as intended (and as popularly understood).

However, if the social contract between state (and/or society) and the corporation cannot be the same as might be proposed between state and citizen (or politically acting natural person), nevertheless the relationship may still be socially contractual even if the (implicit) elements are not the same. This is because when it comes to recognizing rights, citizen (and even person) are categories that are not natural (unlike our practical recognition of someone as a person) but rather are legal and/or socio-political constructions; polities are at liberty to (re)construct them as they see fit.[44] Thus, if we understand incorporation as evidence of this contractual relation, even if currently the public regarding aspects of the contract are downplayed,[45] and the contract cannot logically include protection *from* the state (even if this is how it is often presented), this does suppose some necessary political relationship between states and corporations. Thus, complaints of corporate influence over state policy can only be concerned with the *extent* of that influence not its overall political legitimacy, as that is clearly underpinned by the social contractual relationship.

If this idea of the social contract has some purchase on domestic relations between states and corporations, this is much less the case in global society/politics.[46] As we enter a world in which the possibility of globalized democracy has become increasingly proclaimed, and the (multinational) corporations' supporters argue that its forms and practices are not political but merely technical, its role in governing the global economic sphere (through private law alongside its governance of its own networks and relations) muddies the waters of the citizenship argument somewhat; corporations now appear to be demanding citizenship at the same time that they are also establishing the rules by which they will be governed. Thus, at the global level, the public interest, the treatment of the corporation as a legally constituted individual, and the assumption that it necessarily contributes to economic well-being all need to be subjected to scrutiny and democratic deliberation if business and democracy are to be truly reconciled within a nascent global (democratic) society.

Part of the difficulty is that unlike other "people" the global corporation seems to lack a firm or established location (not least as their activities may be global in character). This allows corporations to escape state-based control in a manner that is unavailable to natural persons because of a number of specific considerations. Firstly, given the economic scale of many corporations' activities and organization, often they can request (and receive) particular and special treatment from states in whose territories they are considering investing, and this is not limited to weak states; legislative competition among states extends to corporations an ability to select the most advantageous jurisdictions in which to locate various aspects of their operations in a way unavailable to others. This ability to select may also extend to the ability to select where cases regarding damages and torts should be adjudicated, again extending a voluntary dimension to corporate personal location. Finally, of course, unlike natural persons, global corporations are complex, multi-faceted, multi-divisional organizations, and as such corporate managers and boards can with some justification regard themselves as "located" in multiple states.[47] This further complicates our perception of the corporate person and further distinguishes them from the natural person on whom their legal rights are modeled.

As I have already noted, incorporation, and the assumption of corporate personality, was originally linked with the notion that such organizations enjoyed this privilege because they undertook to serve the public interest. David Korten has suggested that this legal protection therefore should be foregone when the practices of specific corporations no longer serve this public interest, however defined.[48] Likewise, Joel Bakan has argued that one key mechanism for policing corporate actions that is currently under-recognized is the revocation of corporate charters by regulators.[49] As yet this final sanction has never been deployed against a major corporation, although it is frequently used against smaller companies for all sorts of procedural infractions, although not for what we might regard as social activities that are detrimental to the public realm/domain.

This leads us to the subject of the next two chapters. When we ask how the individual is governed we are asking two linked questions: what are the internal morality and ethical considerations that shape our behavior; and what are the social and legal restraints that we encounter in modern society (and what sanctions are available to ensure compliance with such restraints)? In the next chapter we look at the internal issues for corporations, centered on issues around the global management of the corporation and questions of corporate social responsibility. Then, in the following chapter we will examine the power of the corporation and return to the social and legal constraints that it may encounter in its market and economic activities. In both chapters we will also begin to see the contours of the relationship between the global corporation and global governance come into clear focus.

Notes

1 Laurence Boulle, *The Laws of Globalization: An Introduction* (Alphen aan den Rijn: Kluwer Law International, 2009), 360–361. I have substituted MNCs in this quote for Boule's use of TNCs, which, as set out in the introduction, seems to me to be a term that is less than helpful; in light of the context this substitution does not distort his argument.
2 Katsuhito Iwai, "Persons, Things and Corporations: The Corporate Personality Controversy and Comparative Corporate Governance," *American Journal of Comparative Law* 47, no. 4 (Autumn 1999), 603.
3 Simon Deakin, "The Juridical Nature of the Firm" in *The Sage Handbook of Corporate Governance*, ed. T. Clarke and D. Branson (London: Sage Publications, 2012), 116.
4 Phillip I. Blumberg, *The Multinational Challenge to Corporation Law. The Search for a New Corporate Personality* (New York: Oxford University Press, 1993), 207.
5 Ibid., 209–210.
6 Binda Sahni, "The Interpretation of the Corporate Personality of Transnational Corporations," *Widener Law Journal* 15 no. 1 (2005): 1–45.
7 Certainly there may be some wealthy individuals able to deploy similarly extensive resources to political ends—George Soros, Bill Gates, Oprah Winfrey—but these are exceptions to the general distinction between the resources likely to be available to the corporate person and those available to the natural person.
8 Tom Hadden, *Company Law and Capitalism* (second edition) (London: Weidenfeld and Nicholson, 1977), 110–116.
9 Stephen Wilks, *The Political Power of the Business Corporation* (Cheltenham: Edward Elgar, 2013): 11; David Ciepley, "Beyond Public and Private: Toward a Political Theory of the Corporation," *American Political Science Review* 107, no. 1 (February 2013): 155–156; José E. Alvarez, "Are Corporations 'Subjects' of International Law," *Santa Clara Journal of International Law* 9, no. 1 (2011): 9–11.

10 Ian Goldman and Ronen Palan, "Corporate Citizenship" in *Global Corporate Power* (IPE Yearbook 15) ed. C. May (Boulder, Colo.: Lynne Rienner Publishers, 2006), 190.
11 Andrew Gamble and Gavin Kelly, "The Politics of the Company" in *The Political Economy of the Company*, ed. J. Parkinson, A. Gamble and G. Kelly (Oxford: Hart Publishing, 2000), 30.
12 Wilks, *The Political Power of the Business Corporation*, 10; Paddy Ireland, "Limited liability, shareholder rights and the problem of corporate irresponsibility," *Cambridge Journal of Economics* 34 (2010): 837–856.
13 Leslie Hannah, *The Rise of the Corporate Economy* (London: Methuen [reprinted, London: Routledge], (1976 [2006]), 20–21.
14 Thorstein Veblen, *Absentee Ownership. Business Enterprise in Recent Times: The Case of America* (New York: B.W. Heubsch [reprinted with a new introduction by Marion J. Levy. New Brunswick, N.J.: Transaction Publishers], (1923 [1997]).
15 Ciepley, "Beyond Public and Private."
16 Ireland, "Limited Liability, Shareholder Rights and the Problem of Corporate Irresponsibility," 853.
17 Ciepley, "Beyond Public and Private," 151.
18 James Dempsey, "Corporations and Non-Agential Moral Responsibility," *Journal of Applied Philosophy* 30, no. 4 (2013): 334–350.
19 Ciepley, "Beyond Public and Private," 142.
20 Ireland, "Limited Liability, Shareholder Rights and the Problem of Corporate Irresponsibility," 838.
21 See Karl Polanyi, *The Great Transformation* (Boston, Mass.: Beacon Press 1944 [1957]).
22 Gary Wilson, "From Black Box to Glocalised Player? Corporate Personality in the Twenty-first Century and the Scope of Law's Regulatory Reach," *Northern Ireland Legal Quarterly* 62, no. 4 (2011): 433–449.
23 Andrew Crane, Dirk Matten, and Jeremy Moon, *Corporations and Citizenship* (Cambridge: Cambridge University Press 2008), 27–31.
24 Goldman and Palan, "Corporate Citizenship," 188.
25 Kevin Farnsworth, *Social Versus Corporate Welfare: Competing Needs and Interests within the Welfare State* (Basingstoke: Palgrave Macmillan, 2012).
26 Merja Pentikäinen, "Changing International 'Subjectivity' and Rights and Obligations under International Law – Status of Corporations," *Utrecht Law Review* 8, no. 1 (January 2012), 147; Peter D. Szigeti, "Territorial Bias in International Law: Attribution in State and Corporate Responsibility," *Journal of Transnational Law and Policy* 19 (Spring 2010): 349–354.
27 Steve Russell and Michael J. Gilbert, "Social Control of Transnational Corporations in the Age of Marketocracy," *International Journal of the Sociology of the Law* 30, no. 1 (March 2002): 45.
28 Joseph E. Stiglitz, "Regulating Multinational Corporations: Towards Principles of Cross-Border Legal Frameworks in a Globalized World Balancing Rights with Responsibilities" (2007 Grotius Lecture), *American University International Law Review* 23 (2008): 553–557.
29 Claire Cutler, "Legal Pluralism as the 'Common Sense' of Transnational Capitalism," *Oñati Socio-Legal Series* 3, no. 4 (2013): 719–740.
30 Stiglitz, "Regulating Multinational Corporations," 550–552; 557.
31 Alvarez, "Are Corporations 'Subjects' of International Law," 28.

32 Ibid., 3–4.
33 Ibid., 9; Pentikäinen, "Changing International 'Subjectivity' and Rights," 152.
34 Ibid., 149.
35 Antje K.D. Heyer, "Corporate Complicity under International Criminal Law: A Case for Applying the Rome Statute to Business Behavior," *Human Rights and International Legal Discourse* 6, no. 1 (2012): 17.
36 Interestingly, given the extent and scope of global corporations' activity, it may be possible to regard their own internal codes of conduct as an emerging body of international customary law, to which they can be held by independent judicial, quasi-judicial and social authorities, see: Gregory T. Euteneier, "Towards a Corporate 'Law of Nations': Multinational Enterprises' contributions to Customary International Law," *Tulane Law Review* 82 (December 2007): 758–780. The issue of the recognition of the international legal personhood of the corporation has some clear if contested impact on the manner by which global corporate practices are governed and the establishment of their specific rights and responsibilities under international law, and we will return to this issue in the next chapter.
37 Steve McGuire, "Multinationals and NGOs Amid a Changing Balance of Power," *International Affairs* 89, no. 3 (2013): 703.
38 Olufemi Amao, *Corporate Social Responsibility, Human Rights and the Law: Multinational corporations in developing countries* (Abingdon: Routledge, 2011), 275.
39 Katsuhito Iwai, "Persons, Things and Corporations: The Corporate Personality Controversy and Comparative Corporate Governance" *American Journal of Comparative Law* 47, no. 4 (Autumn 1999): 583–632; David Ciepley (see: Ciepley, "Beyond Public and Private") adopts a similar division of analytical approaches describing the first and second types as associational and entity theories, which are then contrasted unfavorably with the grant theory that I explore when I discuss the grant of rights to corporations by states.
40 Ireland, "Limited Liability, Shareholder Rights and the Problem of Corporate Irresponsibility," 851.
41 David Ciepley, "Neither Persons nor Associations: Against Constitutional Rights for Corporations," *Journal of Law and Courts* 1, no. 2 (Fall 2013): 225; see also Steven Gerenscer, "The Corporate Person and Democratic Politics," *Political Research Quarterly* 58, no. 4 (December 2005): 630.
42 Ciepley, "Neither Persons nor Associations," 231, *emphasis added*.
43 Gerenscer, "The Corporate Person and Democratic Politics," 630.
44 Ibid., 632–634.
45 Joel Bakan, *The Corporation: The Pathological Pursuit of Profit and Power* (New York: Free Press, 2004).
46 Ann Florini, "Global Companies and Global Society: The Evolving Social Contract" in *The Handbook of Global Companies*, ed. J. Mikler (Chichester: John Wiley & Sons, 2013): 335–350.
47 Benedict S. Wray and Rosa Raffaelli, "False Extraterritoriality? Municipal and Multinational Jurisdiction over Transnational Corporations," *Human Rights and International Discourse* 8, no. 1 (2012): 124–125.
48 David C. Korten, *When Corporations Rule the World* (London: Earthscan, 1995), 54.
49 Bakan, *The Corporation*, 156.

3 The governance of corporations

- Governing the corporation
- The shape of corporate governance: management vs. owners?
- Corporate social responsibility
- The United Nations Global Compact
- Conclusion

Global corporations are often complex organizations, and we need to understand how global corporations' own governance is affected by the institutions of global governance specifically, but also how corporate governance might be seen as a form of focused (global) governance in itself. In Chapter 5 I focus on the question of the interaction between national tax regimes and the organization of corporate structures and practices, but in this chapter we start with a range of more general issues before concluding with a short consideration of corporate social responsibility. I should also stress that different corporations, having different interests and being organized differently will have different sets of interactions with the institutions of global governance, and thus the general considerations set out in this and the following chapter would need to be tempered in any specific case by an examination of how these general issues play out. Thus, this and the following chapter are intended to provide an analytical agenda which can be deployed in the examination of any particular set of relations between a corporation and the mechanism/practices of global governance.

At the heart of any consideration of the governance of corporations is a tension between the understandable corporate interest in profitability or other strategic aims (such as access to new markets, or the development of new technologies) and the costs that governance-related compliance may introduce. Especially when the focus is on how corporate governance should protect and enhance shareholder value, the costs of compliance with any legal and quasi-legal requirements introduced by various aspects of (global) governance may result in difficult-to-resolve dilemmas for corporate boards and managers, with solutions varying between corporations. The privileging of shareholder value (either actually or as a proxy) also may have costs as regards the prosecution of a longer term strategy of investment, but which may have a shareholder pay-off if successfully achieved and concluded.

Corporations and their commercial predecessors have always required some form of governance although the term itself is of a relatively recent vintage (only becoming common in its now most frequently understood meaning in the 1980s). Moreover, while initially limited to the relationship between investors and the corporation (and the management of that relationship), contemporary perspectives on corporate governance tend to accept that corporate decisions and practices have impact far beyond the shareholders. Thus, one way of understanding states' interest in the legal regulation of corporate governance is to see it as a continuing dialectic relationship between the recognition of the social impact of corporate practices and the demand for forms of state regulation to encourage, ameliorate, and control (or even prevent) such practices. Oversight of corporate governance has been about shaping corporate activity towards valued ends, not only prompted by that which might be deemed socially unacceptable or damaging in some way. Conversely, one can see the move to reform corporate governance as a reflection of the financialization of the global political economy, which is to say that it reflects the move to a mode of corporate control that rests on the utilization of financial data and instruments. Thus, powerful financial institutions have had a clear interest in maintaining and expanding the protections for shareholders, and developing a large liquid securities or stock market, enabling them to mobilize their financial control to restructure corporations in the interest of maximizing returns while also underpinning such developments through the sector's service provision—from mergers and acquisitions consultancy to the provision of "helpful" financial instruments to support such restructuring.[1] Reform of corporate governance has not only been focused on its financial aspects; it is also the method of control (via financial metrics and mechanisms) that has been characteristic of contemporary ownership.

Since the 1980s the interest in corporate governance, especially in the United Kingdom and United States has led to a proliferation of reports on improving corporate governance and an ever expanding set of codes of conduct to encourage preferred behavior; this has had considerable impact across the global political economy prompting the Organisation for Economic Co-operation and Development (OECD) to also establish a set of guidelines for its members developing their own codes, building on the various national developments.[2] However, especially at the global level, because of the limitations of international law as regards corporations (as discussed earlier), much of the global governance of corporate governance remains in the forms of such guidelines, while in national jurisdictions there is considerably more scope for formal regulation. Between these two levels the European Union has focused more on establishing an "efficient" European market for corporate ownership rather than seeking to harmonize company law across the EU.

Perhaps most obviously the 2007 EU Directive on *Fostering an Appropriate Regime for Shareholders' Rights* focused on issues around transparency and the availability of corporate data to facilitate decision-making by potential investors; the regulation of corporate governance here is intended to serve the needs of those seeking to invest in the corporate sector.[3] Moreover in a series of judgments around the turn of the millennium, the European Court of Justice (ECJ) established a competitive environment for incorporation by upholding corporations' rights to incorporate in whatever EU jurisdiction best served their needs and for their (centralized) corporate governance to be regulated by the home law of that member.[4] However, this also means that despite operating in an EU member's jurisdiction a non-domiciled corporation is not necessarily subject to that state's regulations on corporate governance, reflecting the more general problem for state-based regulation where "rights of establishment" for corporations seldom include a requirement for local incorporation as well, although for other reasons subsidiaries are often incorporated in the host state.[5] The global regulation of corporate governance (especially in the EU) combines three levels of governance: the domestic/home state; any regional agreement; and the global level which consists of guidelines and principles.

As one might imagine there is an interesting relationship between these differing forms and levels of regulation that remains uncertain and potentially incomplete. Moreover, in different jurisdictions local (national) politics will deliver different political responses to the question of how to regulate corporate governance. On one side we might expect convergence around methods of corporate governance preferred by financial market participants as the market for corporate ownership is itself increasingly globalized, but on the other given the continuing dependence on national legal systems, we might also expect some continued diversity where financial sectors are perhaps not as influential. There is an argument that market competition of the type underpinned by the ECJ's judgments could prompt convergence, but this is likely still to be balanced by national political trajectories and developments.[6]

Governing the corporation

There is some debate about whether differences between common law and civil law traditions or institutions have prompted different paths for the development of corporate governance across the global system, although continuing research indicates that there is more variation than even a two traditions approach suggests, with considerable divergence in some areas of the regulation of the governance of corporations.[7] Nevertheless, generally corporate governance is usually taken to cover company, securities, and labor relations law in addition to the general laws applicable to economic activity (such as property law or contract law) in any given society. As Masahiko Aoki puts it:

> [F]or business corporations to become an institutionalized element of a social order, stable expectations need to be both generated and sustained in a society in terms of the patterns of corporate behavior. In other words, corporate governance must be such as to generate corporate behavior that is largely consistent and coherent with institutional arrangements.[8]

As this might imply, the role (and form) of government may have some impact on how various aspects of corporate governance develop; Mark Roe suggests that the more developed a state's social democratic character, the more likely that corporate governance will include substantial non-financial dimensions.[9] Social democracies are more likely to seek to intercede between the managers and owners to promote the interests of other stakeholders (often but by no means exclusively, the corporation's workforce).

This is not to say that corporations merely respond to an existing environment; as we will explore later the corporate sector may be able to shift the normative environment so that social consistency is achieved through movements in the general social appreciation of modes of business rather than amendment of these modes of behavior themselves. Nevertheless, mostly corporate governance explicitly focuses on a range of topics including:

- *The composition of the corporation's board of directors*, most explicitly the balance between executive and non-executive directors (those that are working within the corporation itself and those who are independent of the internal management).The key issue here is usually the question of having independent views about corporate strategy and activity to contrast with those of the senior managers who may have differing priorities from the shareholders/owners.

- *The introduction of independent audit committees* to examine and control the regular independent auditing of the corporation's financial reporting. Given the complex character of corporate financial reports, there is considerable potential for bad news to be "buried" alongside the manipulation of data to present (perhaps) misleading impressions to the reader of annual reports. The independent audit committee is intended as an initial independent reviewer of figures in advance of the formal annual audit.

- *The roles and division of labor between the chairman of the board of directors and the chief executive officer (CEO) of the corporation.* Considerable experience suggests that it is seldom advisable to have these two roles shared by one person, although it is not unusual, especially with powerful (charismatic) corporate leaders that the roles are combined. The sharing of the role can greatly compromise the ability of the board to hold senior managers to account as the chair of the board is likely to be able to control the agenda of board meetings and shape the membership of the board to further their particular interests (if they are also CEO).

- *The role and practice of remuneration committees* (an issue that in the period after the financial crisis of 2008 has become of much wider interest than previously). One major recent concern here has been the self-reinforcing acceleration of senior managerial pay. Remuneration committees are often drawn from a relatively small pool of "independent" directors and it is often suspected that these directors (in their own interests) seek to maintain high pay levels for executives rather than address concerns about inequality of pay within corporations or between senior executives and other workers more generally.

- *The practice and utilization of various forms of compensation and incentivization* to manage the performance of senior managers (from bonuses and the role of share options to "golden handshakes" and "golden parachutes"). In the wake of the 2008 financial crisis there is a widespread concern that the use of various forms of reward has encouraged excessive risk taking and short-term management decisions.[10]

- *The recruitment (nomination) of new board members*, including the range of candidates, their induction and their terms/periods of office and the range of expertise available on the board (recently this has been especially focused on boards including at least one director with detailed financial experience) alongside the clear allocation of oversight responsibilities. Recent examples have suggested that some directors have little independent ability (or competence) to interrogate managers' claims and statements to the board. In recent corporate scandals it has sometimes seemed that some board members have been unaware of aspects of the corporation's activity that should have been possible to discern from materials available to them. Additionally, there is a growing suspicion that the narrow range of people recruited to boards can result in a form of group-think where basic presumptions about corporate practices are not critically scrutinized.[11]

- *The responsibilities of the board* as regards corporate behavior including the development of internal codes of best practice and the corporation's compliance with such codes. It is sometimes the case that boards have taken a relatively narrow view of their responsibilities, often merely focusing on the maximization of shareholder value (see below). Many codes of conduct seek to encourage (or require) boards take a much wider view of their oversight of the manner in which the corporation conducts its affairs, to include the development of internal codes of conduct and new mechanisms to gauge compliance with such codes, and importantly the role of civil regulation (again to which we return to below).

- *The range and presentation of information and data in annual reports.* There has been considerable interest in making annual reports clearer and thus more accessible to individual "retail" investors. This also recognizes that for many the only way of finding out what the corporation is doing is via its annual report with its legal constraints (rather than via corporate websites, which are focused much more on marketing and impression management).

- *The manner of liaison with shareholders,* including the practices and influence of shareholder votes at annual general meetings (AGMs). There has been a move recently to legalize binding shareholder votes over some issues at AGMs. This is most developed on issues of remuneration and nomination of directors, but there is a tendency for corporations to pre-confer with large institutional shareholders, and ride out any criticisms or views of small shareholders during the AGM. To some extent concerns around shareholder liaison are about bringing shareholders and managers more closely in contact (which is not necessarily welcomed by senior managers).

As is clear from this (long but still partial) list, the interest in corporate governance focuses mostly on the level of the board and its relationship with senior managers, who are regarded as broadly responsible for the practices and behavior of all staff of the corporation. This range of concerns is subject to two forms of regulation or governance. Firstly, there are the formal legal constraints on practices which are established in national legislation; secondly, there are the demands of shareholders and others that may be articulated via non-legal means and are more about reputational impact.

Given the role of national legislation in the regulation of (and structuring of) corporate governance there is also a political dimension to the issue. However, what causes much comment, and over which opinion differs, is the direction of influence between companies and the state as regards the regulation of corporations generally, and specifically the role of the state as regards corporate governance.[12] We will come back to this, but here I note that across Europe at least, significant aspects of corporate governance have been increasingly harmonized through the work of the European Union and its ability to promote the convergence of economic regulation around common (or parallel) legal instruments.

The shape of corporate governance: management vs. owners?

Problems in corporate governance are usually thought of as principal-agent issues: the shareholders are the principals trying to ensure the managers, their agents, work to their (the principals') interest not their (the agents') own. Solutions are then often specified as a strengthening of shareholder (legal) rights. This can often be in tension with other proposed and actual regulatory developments that seek to strengthen the rights of a range of other internal (workforce) and external (civil society) stakeholders. Indeed in European regulation there has been a clear shift towards the prioritization of the shareholders,[13] but even so the directors as managers have a variety of legal powers to act on behalf of the corporation (or indeed to act *as* the corporation), not least of all by exercising their overall decision-making function on a day-to-day basis.

Therefore, one of the most important legal tensions around the corporation is the manner in which the relationship between shareholder and corporation is treated; especially in the common law tradition, there is some difficulty fixing this relationship. Company law in many jurisdictions has sought to separate (through corporate personality and limited liability) the shareholders *qua* owners from the corporation as legal entity. The property of the corporation is lodged with the corporation not the putative owners, while the managers are employed by the corporation and not the shareholders. However, much is also made of the fiduciary duties of directors to serve the interests of the shareholders, and perhaps most obviously the focus on maximizing "shareholder value" as the priority for corporate boards.[14] Therefore, at the heart of the question of corporate governance and its regulation is a contradiction, which, while perhaps under-remarked, requires the regulation of corporate governance to face in two different directions. The expansion of the market for corporate control has given shareholders a clear set of mechanisms to influence the board, through the ability to expand (or decrease) their holdings almost at will, and (at least) partly enforce a concentration on shareholder value, while at the same time most company law (in most developed jurisdictions, at least) continues to treat the corporation as an autonomous self-governing organization completely separate from any responsibility of its owners for its actions, with legal responsibilities as regards its conduct.

Historically there has been a long-term decline in the ownership of shares by individual investors. At least part of this trend has been through the development of pension fund investing and thus the mediation of individual investment by various financial intermediaries. With the exception of a small cadre of wealthy individuals who are able to assemble major shareholdings in corporations, in the main when we look at the relationship between the owners and managers of corporations we are looking at the relationship between two sets of institutions or organizations. The character of a relationship between two sets of institutions has encouraged the focus on specific metrics to gauge performance (although this is also the result of other factors as well). Institutional investors are often handling a potentially large range of investments, and have little interest in the actual practices of "their" companies other than how their results feed into the general achievements of the managed investment fund, although there are also some activist fund managers who do take a more proactive interest in their holdings. The most obvious of these metrics for the management of shareholdings is what we have been referring to as "shareholder value."

The idea that corporate strategy should be focused on maximizing shareholder value finds it origins in the late 1970s and early 1980s in the United States and United Kingdom. As the market for shares became more dominated by institutional shareholders, so their willingness to cash in investments (to reinvest) and their "need" to report rises in value of their holdings (for competitive and marketing reasons) prompted a fluid market in corporate control to be developed. This shift was at least partly caused by the move on Wall Street from supporting long-term corporate activity through the bond issuance, to more active (fee generating) merger and acquisition support.[15] This shift, which was also influenced by the rise of the New Right's view of how economies should be managed, has often been characterized as the "financialization" of capitalism. William Lazonick and Mary O'Sullivan summarize these moves in the run up to the turn of the millennium thus:

> In the name of 'creating shareholder value', the past two decades have witnessed a marked shift in the strategic orientation of top corporate managers in the allocation of corporate resources and returns away from 'retain and reinvest' and towards 'downsize and distribute'. Under the new regime, top managers downsize the corporations they control, with a particular emphasis on cutting the size of the labor forces they employ, in an attempt to increase the return on equity.[16]

It is this return on equity that is a key metric for the distant institutional investor who may have little detailed knowledge of the corporation in which they have invested, but will understand comparative financial data very well. Thus, unsurprisingly corporate managers started to focus on the forms of activity (and financial manipulation) that would maximize their stock price, especially as stock options and other share-based incentive plans tied their remuneration more closely to the share price of the corporations they managed, a trend that was already well developed at the beginning of the period of financialization but was accelerated by it.[17] As this suggests one element of corporate governance is intended to solve the principal-agent issue, to ensure the managers of corporations are focused on the interests of their putative owners, and not on their own bureaucratic-organizational interests in expanding the resources under their control. This is, however, a rather thin depiction of the contemporary governance of corporate practices, and despite the European work on regional governance of corporate governance, perhaps underplays the exposure of the internal workings of global corporations to global governance.

Corporate social responsibility

Famously, Milton Friedman argued in 1970 that the only social responsibility of the corporation was to make a profit for its shareholders; while there might be other social benefits to corporate activity, these were incidental to this primary concern.[18] Indeed Friedman argued on a broadly utilitarian basis that by maximizing the profit/return on investment, the corporation's incidental social benefit would be maximized, and is partly how the expansion of shareholder value as a key metric of evaluation of corporate success has been justified. It also prompted two different (but perhaps complementary) responses as regards the social impact of corporate activity: one is that shareholder value is best served by the corporation being attuned to its social responsibilities, not least as brand reputation, stemming from these activities may have a direct effect on the bottom line; alternatively, Friedman's view is too thin a view of the corporation's social role, disregarding the social benefits accruing from state instituted incorporation and the subsequent social responsibility to balance the receipt of such benefits. Either way, corporations' behaviour and practices are now a legitimate concern for governance, with considerable interest shown in the new millennium in finding ways for corporations to be held to account for the social impact of their activity, most often articulated under the rubric corporate social responsibility.

Corporate social responsibility (CSR), by virtue of the range of corporate activity and practice it might be said to encompass, is necessarily a complex concept; as it is also evaluative and freighted with considerable political meaning (both positively and negatively), establishing a consensual definition continues to be difficult.[19] Certainly, most if not all definitions of CSR focus on corporate behavior and/or practices—on what corporations *actually* do beyond any claim(s) they may make. However, for some this primarily concerns their impact on the environment, while for others it encompasses labor and workforce relations, or cultural impact, or a social role beyond their core commercial sphere. While motivation is of some interest, by focusing mostly on actions, discussions of CSR are often relatively ambivalent about why corporations may seek to develop a clear CSR policy.[20] Certainly some may see CSR as essentially a signaling function, to consumers (around brand differentiation), to workers (to attract and retain certain sorts of prospective employees) and to governments (to forestall more legalistic and formal regulation); corporations adopting CSR are trying to say something about themselves even if some critics regard such invocations of social responsibility as being articulated in bad faith, and a mask for the operation of a rapacious global capitalism.[21] Indeed we might say that the assessment of risk has moved from a primary concern with impact of actions on others, to a concern for the risk that the *publicity* around adverse impacts may have economic costs to the corporation itself. Where this corporate-risk aspect becomes central, critics understandably see CSR as merely marketing or a cynical interest in brand values. However, equally Naomi Klein and others have identified this brand vulnerability as one way to "encourage" corporations towards more responsible behavior.[22]

To make some sense of the range of approaches to CSR, we can follow Adaeze Okoye who identifies four streams of approach to defining CSR:

- instrumental theories advancing social objectives through economic activities;
- political theories advocating corporate power and its responsible use;
- integrative theories expressing the necessity for corporations to integrate social demands; and
- ethical theories examining the morality and rightness of corporate social action.[23]

The first is the Friedmanite position that the social impact of corporate practice is outside the concern of the corporation other than how preferences are articulated through the market, and how the legal structures of regulation are framed by politically competent and legitimate authority. The second set of approaches is concerned with the notion of good corporate citizenship and might be regarded as likely to go little further than suggesting that, like all citizens, corporations might be best advised to follow both the letter and the spirit of the law. If there is a difference here, it is around the corporate understanding (self-reflection) of its social impact within the legal regulatory regime (and as such might be regarded as suggesting aggressive tax planning is socially suspect). Both these approaches de-radicalize CSR through a focus on markets and legal compliance. However, many supporters of CSR seek very different ends from these, and, thus, for our purposes, the latter two clusters of ideas are more fruitful; in both, CSR goes beyond the demands of legislation and regulation to articulate through action(s) a response to the interests of non-corporate stakeholders.

For integrative approaches the key issue is recognizing the responsibility of the corporation for the impact of its practices on the welfare and/or interests of various stakeholders within and outside its organizational scope. Here the development of global supply chains has expanded the realm in which the centrally coordinating corporation can find itself exposed to claims of irresponsibility or complicity in unwelcome impacts. This can be understood as a shift from a direct legal way of conceiving corporate responsibility to one that is more focused on modes of social connection.[24] This shift requires a forward-looking attention to potential solutions to emerging issues rather than the previous backward-looking focus on strict liability. Here standards setting organizations such as Fairtrade organizations and sustainable sourcing certification regimes (such as the Forest Stewardship Council) play a key role, with the corporation's managers taking a more proactive interest in how their network(s) is/are governed.

Ethical approaches are in a sense more evaluative, in that they seek to establish the forms of behavior and practice that would support the further development (and maintenance) of the good society, often building on proposed general norms such as human rights, principles of environmental sustainability, or the rule of law. Here the legitimacy of corporate activity and practice becomes subject to debate and argument by those wishing to question the moral legitimacy of particular outcomes (measured against a standard proposed as universal), and perhaps most importantly, while corporations may be interlocutors in such arguments, often it is the judgment of those deemed to be independent that carries the greatest social evaluative weight. This can result in campaigns to boycott specific corporations, particular products/goods or "naming and shaming" of practices critics identify as irresponsible, whatever their legal status. However, here the issue of moral legitimacy is double-edged as both the legitimacy of the corporation, *and* that of those who seek to evaluate corporate behavior are in play. Whether the focus is on environmental degradation and sustainability, on workers' rights, human rights, global corporations' political role in host states, or on wider concerns around their socio-cultural influence, the legitimacy of those seeking to hold corporations to account is as important as the activity being judged.[25]

More problematic is the question of whether the corporation (as a legally constituted individual) can be regarded as a repository of moral responsibility; is the corporation a moral agent?[26] On one hand, given the earlier discussion of corporate personhood one might regard this responsibility as a balancing item for the rights corporations have gained through personhood. Conversely, given the focus on the morality of actions, CSR in the end may collapse into the moral responsibility of those who work within the corporation, and thus "piercing the corporate veil" would be a key mechanism for assigning moral responsibility for the actions of the corporation. This second approach would indicate that non-corporate focused social regulation (legal and normative) remains salient, but given my focus on corporations I will here retain the focus on the corporation as an ethical "citizen" in global politics.

In whatever way we seek to define CSR, in the end it seems clear that consumers pay the costs of these practices, through higher prices for products and services, but for many this is a market choice, clearly labeled and signaled by the corporation itself. The main reason for this form of cost recovery is that while CSR may not necessarily therefore reduce margins, it has little demonstrable impact on financial performance—it offers little market advantage.[27] Conversely the interest in CSR may be about leveling the playing field; where corporations from developing countries are able to deploy a cost advantage, CSR gives developed country competitors a lever to criticize these low-cost market entrants as failing to encompass standards that have been politically endorsed in developed countries and more widely.[28] The continuing expansion of CSR both as rhetoric and practice may also be tied to the increasingly political role of global corporations, which in turn exposes them to more extensive interest in their activities; as corporations engage more openly with political processes (through lobbying/influence, but also by delivering services via the privatization of state functions), questions about their social standing, including CSR, play an increased part in the discourse around domestic and global politics.[29] This has not, however, been matched by any major expansion in formal (as opposed to voluntary) modes of compliance monitoring over and above those required by domestic company law (including those related to corporate governance) or, perhaps more importantly, by any framework for sanctioning non-compliance. Nevertheless, the increased political visibility of CSR-related issues has prompted a number of attempts to formulate a general (and global) set of principles on which most if not all parties might agree.

During the 1970s, partly as a response to the increasingly visible global scope of operations of many corporations, there were moves to develop a global set of guidelines or principles for corporate practice. For instance, in response to the political debates around the legitimacy or otherwise of trading with apartheid South Africa, Leon Sullivan (a US Baptist preacher, civil rights leader and member of the General Motors board) proposed a private code of conduct for 12 US multinationals operating in that country. The seven principles covered issues primarily around inter-racial labor relations and were intended to encourage corporations working in South Africa to demand full integration of the black population into management, training, and work opportunities into their operations. Around the same time, and with a more general focus, the OECD published its own set of principles, most recently updated in 2011. The guidelines cover issues of disclosure, human rights, employment and industrial relations issues, impact on the environment, combating bribery (including measures on the solicitation of bribes as well as extortion), consumer interests, issues around the sharing of science and technology, the regulation of competition, and the responsible payment of tax.[30] Additionally, in the 1970s and 1980s the relatively short-lived UN Centre on Transnational Corporations (which eventually was subsumed into the UN Conference on Trade and Development—UNCTAD) worked towards a more exacting code of conduct but this was never fully achieved, although the effort was (implicitly) revived in the development of the UN Norms on the Responsibilities of TNCs and Other Business Enterprises. The UN Norms divided responsibilities between corporations or commercial organizations and states, leaving significant opportunity for gaming the division and as such failed to have much impact.[31] Conversely, the seeds planted by UNCTC's efforts and the ongoing debates about the most appropriate methods for regulating global corporate conduct have also prompted the establishment of the United Nations Global Compact (UNGC), to which I now turn.

The United Nations Global Compact

In 2012 there were just under 7,000 businesses who were current members of the UNGC, although there is a certain amount of churn partly because of the increasingly rigorous examination of members' self-reporting. Thus, in June 2012 while 104 companies of various sizes joined the compact, 100 members were removed from the active list for failure to submit acceptable self-reflexive reports on their progression towards the compact's preferred modes of behavior as expressed in the compact's principles.[32] The secretariat of the Global Compact presents its ten principles as clearly related to the wider norms encompassed by the United Nations, and seeks to encourage a wide range of commercial organizations seeking to promote these principles to examine the fit between them and corporations' *actual* practices.

Box 3.1. United Nations Global Compact: Ten Principles

The UN Global Compact's ten principles in the areas of human rights, labor, the environment, and anti-corruption enjoy universal consensus and are derived from:

The Universal Declaration of Human Rights
The International Labour Organization's Declaration on Fundamental Principles and Rights at Work

The Rio Declaration on Environment and Development
The United Nations Convention Against Corruption
The UN Global Compact asks companies to embrace, support, and enact, within their sphere of influence, a set of core values in the areas of human rights, labor standards, the environment, and anti-corruption:

Human rights

Principle 1: Businesses should support and respect the protection of internationally proclaimed human rights; and
Principle 2: make sure that they are not complicit in human rights abuses.

Labor

Principle 3: Businesses should uphold the freedom of association and the effective recognition of the right to collective bargaining;
Principle 4: the elimination of all forms of forced and compulsory labor;
Principle 5: the effective abolition of child labor; and
Principle 6: the elimination of discrimination in respect of employment and occupation.

Environment

Principle 7: Businesses should support a precautionary approach to environmental challenges;
Principle 8: undertake initiatives to promote greater environmental responsibility; and
Principle 9: encourage the development and diffusion of environmentally friendly technologies.

Anti-corruption

Principle 10: Businesses should work against corruption in all its forms, including extortion and bribery.
Source: United Nations Global Compact 'About Us.'[33]

The Compact contains four mechanisms through which the modification of corporate practices may be achieved: Dialogue; Learning; Projects; and Local Networks. Policy Dialogues bring together corporate managers with representatives of various labor and civil society groups, to work with governments on the development of policies to further the aims of the compact. The Learning Forum is intended to allow (through its website and at meetings) the sharing of experiences and the identification of "knowledge gaps" between the best practice of compact participants and those seeking advice on how to improve their own practices. Partnership projects provide opportunities for groups (specifically among the "poor") to develop research and advocacy projects related to corporate activities, again publicized through a website. Finally, the Global Compact explicitly supports outreach efforts to establish and maintain local networks, through which its aims can be articulated and supported by civil society. Overall, therefore, the compact is facilitative of political action, but is predicated on a central role for corporations themselves: it is an inclusive forum, rather than an external regulatory mechanism.

Indeed, some commentators have argued that the compact has enabled corporations to "blue wash" their activities by claiming an association with the UN (and by extension its values and norms) while not fundamentally changing their behavior. As Jackie Smith sums up this critique:

> The Global Compact is ultimately an arrangement that privatizes relations between the UN and transnational corporations, thereby insulating corporations from public scrutiny while tying the hands of the UN, thereby limiting its capacities to ensure implementation of international law and norms.[34]

Certainly this sort of criticism is not uncommon, prompting some shifts in its organizational practices and demands including new conditions on the use of the compact's logo, and stricter rules on how partners communicate their progress towards the compact's goals.[35] However, many of the compact's supporters argue that the norms it encompasses have had some clear influence over contemporary corporate behavior. There is some evidence for instance that there has been some convergence in CSR reporting by compact members which enhances the ability to make comparative judgments and identify those moving fastest towards high levels of norm acceptance and compliance.[36] Indeed, this was more its intent—to act as a moral compass for global business—rather than to provide a regulatory regime with formalized verification standards; the compact was and is intended by its originators to shift the understanding of corporate (social) responsibilities and act as a socializing complement to other forms of regulation.[37] This is to say that much of the criticism of the UNGC misunderstands its intent and criticizes it for not doing what it was never actually intended to accomplish.

If the Global Compact itself is intended to change corporate behavior through socialization, normative education and other forms of "encouragement," one might infer that the issue of monitoring actual compliance with its various strictures has been assigned to civil regulation, while the implementation of change is left to the corporate members themselves. This is not to say that it has been privatized in the sense of hidden away, but rather that the measurement and assessment of compliance has been passed to non-governmental organizations (NGOs) who act to publicize both good behavior (via certification schemes and awards linked to preferred actions) and publically criticize negative outcomes. Civil regulation has to some extent flowed into the regulatory vacuum created by the disparity in scope of corporate activity and the forms of global governance of corporate activity.[38] Thus, while there are reporting mechanisms within the UNGC, it is largely left to independent NGOs to "police" the behavior on which they focus. Thus, the independent Global Reporting Initiative entered a strategic alliance with the Compact's organization in 2006 (renewed in 2010),[39] and became the favored supplier of detailed guidelines, assessment, and evaluation to UNGC members with a relatively high level of required disclosure.

More generally, civil regulatory forms including groups that examine the UNGC linked corporations alongside certification regimes (such as the Forest Stewardship Council, or various Fairtrade marks) allow a corporation's behavior and practices to be judged against a set of relatively explicit criteria. For the certification focused groups, the implied reputational benefit of successfully being certified and the reputational cost of the civil regulatory regime "naming and shaming" non-compliant members of the scheme can (or should) prompt the modification of behavior. Three sorts of civil regulatory regime that have some impact on corporate practice can be easily identified:

- those that set out substantive norms of behavior and as such are outcome focused. Here corporations accede to a regime such as the UNGC that refers to international agreements and treaties and will publicize failings to fulfill these behavioral norms;
- those that focus more on the procedure by which corporate decisions are reached. The regime will be concerned with compliance with standards for weighing various elements in decisions (the most obvious being environmental impact). Perhaps the most important institution in this form of civil regulation is the International Organization for Standardization based in Geneva; and

- thirdly, there are also reporting initiatives which provide corporations with independent assessment of their activities and practices against various non-financial outcomes. These regimes offer both opportunities for corporations to request assessments, but also sometimes independently report on corporate activity, seeking to apply public pressure for change.[40]

Many regimes combine two or all three of these forms of regulation, but for global corporations, at the very least, some response rooted in corporate governance is required to the articulation of stakeholders' (posited) interests. Thus, if corporate governance has been widened in scope to include a range of non-shareholding stakeholders, the manner in which corporations recognize these interests via the actions of various groups conducting civil regulatory oversight also represents a widening of the structures of the global governance of corporate governance. Indeed, once the corporation is required to manage the behavior and practices of its network and/or supply chain to the agenda(s) set by CSR, its role as an institution of global governance itself starts to come more into focus.

Conclusion

As Stephen Wilkes put it: "corporate governance is too important to be left to shareholders,"[41] and in one sense the (global) social developments discussed above are a response to exactly such a realization. Moreover, if the UNGC has been largely concerned with encouraging or incentivizing responsible behavior as the most fruitful approach, another way of conceiving of the global governance of corporations is to focus on irresponsibility. To some extent this can easily be inferred from the above, with the idea of civil regulation and consumer campaigns as forms of sanctions for socially irresponsible corporate practice. Indeed, given the relative lack of "hard" global governance around the behavior and practices of corporations, it is perhaps understandable that there have been attempts to establish extraterritorial reach for laws governing corporations' domestic activities. The most often cited example of this (albeit limited) trend is the US Alien Torts Claims Act (ATCA), which has allowed alleged victims of human rights abuses outside the United States to sue corporations in US courts. While a number of cases have been brought under this provision, and in a couple of cases corporations have settled in advance of judgment, currently there has been no successful prosecution of a corporation under the act, despite the hopes often articulated by critics of corporate behavior. Interestingly, while many lobbyists have disputed the legitimacy of ACTA's provisions as regards corporations, when extraterritorial considerations have been included in bilateral investment treaties as protection for inwards investors' property rights, there has been broad support from the same lobbyists.[42] This asymmetry will be returned to in the next chapter, but these attempts to assert extraterritorial jurisdiction clearly contradict the international legal norm of sovereign equality (by asserting one state's law over another's jurisdiction) and as such could be regarded as compromising the potential for formally legal based global governance of such issues.

Indeed, as I have already noted, the story of the global governance of corporations has been presented in some critical accounts as a two-sided development: the increasing robustness of cross-border protections of corporate property and shareholders' rights; and the retention of a soft, and in the last analysis voluntary, approach to corporate responsibilities. This asymmetry is unlikely to be accidental and as such for critics of the global corporate economy, it is directly indicative of the strength and extent of global corporate political power. Indeed, such developments are often perceived as thwarting political will towards more formal legal regulatory mechanisms, perhaps ignoring the fact that such a move at the international level would require a legal "revolution" to make corporate entities recognized subjects of international law. Moreover, if one presumes that much corporate activity is driven by the market environment in which they operate, suggesting changes short of reforming capitalism itself may in the end be quixotic.

Even leaving aside a revolutionary moment, in one sense the discussion above may undermine the previous chapter's emphasis on corporate personality, as following the above discussion, one might conclude that there is insufficient (global) legal ground on which the global corporation as legal person might stand. Conversely, it may be more useful to accept that while there are clearly some legal difficulties, corporations' own perception of their personality is sufficient reason to use this as a practical way into the discussion of governance. Moreover, although we might expect globalization in one form or another to encourage a convergence of corporate governance regimes' regulatory focus and method, national jurisdictional particularities (and political economic histories) continue to shape and pattern corporate governance, even if these converge on a similar set of issues to resolve.

Certainly there are aspects of global market regulation that have converged, perhaps most obviously around intellectual property rights,[43] but in other realms the recourse to civil regulation and the

UN Global Compact reflect not convergence but rather the lack thereof.[44] Thus even in the wake of a financial crisis that demonstrated the reality of global economic contagion, the regulation of corporate governance while certainly exposed to various forms of relatively soft global governance has seen little (what we might refer to as) hard global convergence. This has been contrary to the expectations around the turn of millennium that supposed enhanced global competition in the corporate sector would work to drive corporations to converge on the most efficient form of corporate governance.[45] Conversely, even before the crisis of 2008, a contrary position saw the continuance of states' ability to regulate (alongside corporations' ability to influence states' policy) as likely supporting continued differentiation in regulatory regimes.[46] Thus, despite the global economic crisis, that the relationship between the global corporate sector and global governance remains fragmented and far from any form of even partial regulatory consolidation, many believe is because of the political power of global corporations.

Notes

1 John W. Cioffi, *Public Law and Private Power: Corporate Governance Reform in the Age of Finance Capitalism* (Ithaca, NY: Cornell University Press, 2010), 22–23.
2 R.I. (Bob) Ticker, "The Evolution of Corporate Governance" in *The Sage Handbook of Corporate Governance*, eds T. Clarke and D. Branson (London: Sage Publications, 2012), 41–48.
3 Laura Horn, *Regulating Corporate Governance in the EU: Towards a Marketization of Corporate Control* (Basingstoke: Palgrave Macmillan, 2012), 130.
4 Ibid., 134–135.
5 Joseph E. Stiglitz, "Regulating Multinational Corporations: Towards Principles of Cross-Border Legal Frameworks in a Globalized World Balancing Rights with Responsibilities" (2007 Grotius Lecture), *American University International Law Review* 23 (2008): 509–510.
6 For a fine grained and well-developed assessment of these issues see: Peter A. Gourevitch and James Shinn, *Political Power and Corporate Control: The New Global Politics of Corporate Governance* (Princeton, N.J.: Princeton University Press, 2005); for an often cited argument from 2000 on the convergence of corporate law, see: Henry Hansmann and Reinier Kraakman, *The End of History for Corporate Law* (Yale Law School Law and Economics Working Paper no. 235) (New Haven, Conn.: Yale Law School, 2000).
7 Masahiko Aoki, *Corporations in Evolving Diversity: Cognition, Governance and Institutions* (Oxford: Oxford University Press, 2010), 71–72.
8 Ibid., 12.

80   *Governance of corporations*

9   Mark J. Roe, *Political Determinants of Corporate Governance: Political Context, Corporate Impact* (Oxford: Oxford University Press, 2003).
10   For instance see: William Lazonick, "In the Name of Shareholder Value: How Executive Pay and Stock Buybacks are Damaging the US Economy" in *The Sage Handbook of Corporate Governance*, ed. T. Clarke and D. Branson (London: Sage Publications, 2012), 476–495; Andrew Smithers, *The Road to Recovery: How and Why Economic Policy Must Change* (Chichester: John Wiley, 2013).
11   See: Sabina Nilesen, "Diversity among Senior Executives and Board Directors" in *The Sage Handbook of Corporate Governance*, ed. T. Clarke and D. Branson (London: Sage Publications, 2012), 345–361.
12   Aoki, *Corporations in Evolving Diversity*, 73.
13   Horn, *Regulating Corporate Governance in the EU.*
14   Paddy Ireland, "Company Law and the Myth of Shareholder Ownership," *Modern Law Review* 62, no. 1 (January 1999): 48.
15   William Lazonick and Mary O'Sullivan, "Maximizing Shareholder Value: A New Ideology for Corporate Governance" *Economy and Society* 29, no. 1 (February 2000): 16.
16   Ibid., 18.
17   Ibid., 25.
18   Markus Kitzmueller and Jay Shimshack, "Economic Perspectives on Corporate Social Responsibility," *Journal of Economic Literature* 50, no. 1 (2012): 52.
19   Adaeze Okoye, "Theorizing Corporate Social Responsibility as an Essentially Contested Concept: Is a Definition Necessary?" *Journal of Business Ethics* 89, no. 4 (2009): 613–627. While Okoye develops an argument at some length that CSR is an "essentially contested concept," space precludes a detailed exploration of this point, although the analysis in this section proceeds on the basis that CSR is such a concept.
20   Kitzmueller and Shimshack, "Economic Perspectives on Corporate Social Responsibility," 54.
21   Leslie Sklair and David Miller, "Capitalist Globalization, Corporate Social Responsibility and Social Policy," *Critical Social Policy* 30, no. 4 (2010): 1–24.
22   Naomi Klein, *No Logo* (London: Flamingo, 2001).
23   Okoye, "Theorizing Corporate Social Responsibility as an Essentially Contested Concept," 614–615.
24   Andreas Georg Scherer and Guido Palazzo, "The New Political Role of Business in a Globalized World: A Review of a New Perspective on CSR and its Implications for the Firm, Governance and Democracy," *Journal of Management Studies* 48, no. 4 (June 2011): 913.
25   At the time of writing (Summer 2014) Fairtrade was being criticized for the lack of substantive benefit to coffee workers from Fairtrade certification; workers in non-certified coffee companies were (allegedly) receiving higher wages, while the extra returns from Fairtrade pricing were being captured by managers and not workers in certified firms. See: *The Observer* "Harsh truths are necessary if Fairtrade is to change the lives of the desperately poor: Consumers need to know who benefits from projects supported by the premium they pay," 25 May 2014, 6.
26   Camilla Maclean and Colin Crouch, "Introduction: The Economic, Political and Ethical Challenges of Corporate Social Responsibility" in *The*

Responsible Corporation in a Global Economy, ed. C. Crouch and C. Maclean (Oxford: Oxford University Press, 2011), 24–25.

27 Kitzmueller and Shimshack, "Economic Perspectives on Corporate Social Responsibility," 78.

28 Robert James Hanlon, "Engineering Corporate Social Responsibility: Elite Stakeholders, States and the Resilience of Neoliberalism," *Contemporary Politics* 17, no. 1 (March 2011): 82.

29 Ibid.; Stephen Wilks, *The Political Power of the Business Corporation* (Cheltenham: Edward Elgar, 2013), 216.

30 The full documentation and commentary for the guidelines can be found at http://mneguidelines.oecd.org/.

31 John Gerard Ruggie, *Just Business: Multinational Corporations and Human Rights* (New York: W.W. Norton & Co. 2013), 51; Katarina Weilert, "Taming the Untamable? Transnational Corporations in United Nations Law and Practice" in *Max Planck Yearbook of United Nations Law* (Vol.14) ed. A. von Bogdandy and R. Wolfrum (Leiden: Brill NV, 2010), 489.

32 Van V. Miller, Luis A. Perez-Bates, and Michael J. Pisani, "Global business, Geopolitics and the United Nations Global Compact" in *Handbook on the Geopolitics of Business*, ed. J.M.S. Munoz (Cheltenham: Edward Elgar, 2013), 79.

33 www.unglobalcompact.org/abouttheGC/TheTenPrinciples/index.html.

34 Jackie Smith, "Power, Interests, and the United Nations Global Compact" in *The Challenges of Global Business Authority: Democratic Renewal, Stalemate, or Decay*, ed. T. Porter and K. Ronit (Albany, NY: State University of New York Press, 2010), 89–113.

35 Catia Gregoratti, "The United Nations Global Compact and Development," *Business Regulation and Non-State Actors: Whose standards? Whose development?*, ed. D. Reed, P. Utting, and A. Mukherjee-Reed (London: Routledge, 2012), 102–103.

36 Stephen Chen and Petra Bouvain, "Is Corporate Responsibility Converging? A Comparison of Corporate Responsibility Reporting in the USA, UK, Australia and Germany," *Journal of Business Ethics* 87, Issue 1—supplement (2009): 299–317.

37 Andreas Rasche, "'A Necessary Supplement': What the United Nations Global Compact Is and Is Not," *Business and Society* 48, no. 4 (2009): 511–537; Ruggie, *Just Business*, xxvii.

38 David Vogel, "The Private Regulation of Global Corporate Conduct" in *The Politics of Global Regulation*, ed. W. Mattli and N. Woods (Princeton, N.J.: Princeton University Press, 2009), 151–188; David Vogel, "The Private Regulation of Global Corporate Conduct: Achievements and Limitations," *Business and Society* 49, no. 1 (2010): 68–87.

39 See: www.globalreporting.org/Pages/default.aspx.

40 Kernaghan Webb, "Corporate Citizenship and Private Regulatory Regimes: Understanding New Governance Roles and Functions" in *Corporate Citizenship and New Governance*, ed. I. Pies and P. Koslowski (Dordrecht: Springer, 2011), 49–50.

41 Wilks, *The Political Power of the Business Corporation*, 249.

42 Stiglitz, "Regulating Multinational Corporations," 537; Erika George, "See No Evil? Revisiting Early Visions of the Social Responsibility of Business:

Adolf A. Berle's Contribution to Contemporary Conversations," *Seattle University Law Review* 33, no. 4 (2010): 990–992.

43 Christopher May and Susan Sell, *Intellectual Property Rights: A Critical History* (Boulder, Colo.: Lynne Rienner, 2005).

44 Douglas Branson, "Global Convergence in Corporate Governance? What a Difference 10 Years Make" in *The Sage Handbook of Corporate Governance*, ed. T. Clarke and D. Branson (London: Sage Publications, 2012), 365–378.

45 Mary O'Sullivan, "The political economy of comparative corporate governance," *Review of International Political Economy* 10, no. 1 (2003): 26–28.

46 Ibid., 30–31.

4 Corporations and the exercise of power

- The power of corporations: in general
- The power of corporations: the case of global governance
- Starting to assess the power and influence of corporations in global governance
- Conclusion

This chapter is about the (political) power of global corporations, both in general terms and as related to global governance in particular; as such I set out the analytical tools that will be deployed to address global corporate taxation in the next chapter. As I pointed out in the introduction, accounts of global corporate power that make a comparison between company turnover (gross receipts) and states' gross domestic product (GDP) to argue that some corporations are as powerful as (or even more powerful than) some states are misleading, and do little to illuminate the issue. Here I assemble a more plausible account of how we might appreciate and assess the power and/or influence of global corporations and how this relates to their role in global governance. Let me also be clear about my starting point: as major internationally active organizations, global corporations have legitimate interests to protect or pursue even if we might identify tendencies to over-emphasize these interests, or recognize not infrequent problems of disproportionate and democratically damaging levels of influence. The account of global corporate power set out here can be utilized to evaluate the balance in any particular issue area between justified and problematic influence, which will always be informed by varying assessments of the political legitimacy of global corporations in general.

Firstly, power is always relational; it is part of any relationship between social actors and does not exist in a social vacuum. Therefore, the shape and character of the power of (global) corporations must be at least partly influenced (or even shaped) by the state or other governance structure(s) in which they operate and interact with other social actors. So for instance, where a state's government is responding to social democratic welfare demands (or logic), it may accord less power to corporations by removing some of their political economic freedom to maneuver.[1] Conversely, states' governments driven by a more free-market (corporate friendly) mind-set may accord more latitude to corporations to decide their own fate(s). Globally active corporations often take advantage of such political differences to enhance their ability to act unilaterally by using the perceived benefits that they bring to a state's economy to play one government off against another. Corporations will also appear more powerful when those that they are dealing with adopt (spontaneously or through "encouragement") a similar set of priorities. This leads to the key point of this chapter: corporate power may be related to the resources that corporations can deploy, but it is also crucially reflected in the ability (or otherwise) to set the agenda of decision-making such that those actions that may benefit the business sector are regarded by governing elites as being good policy or common-sense, not merely a particular interest group's preferences.

We can relatively readily infer that corporations (or more accurately their boards and senior managers) seek to deploy what influence and power they may have (or believe they have) to maintain and expand their profitability. However, this may not be necessarily the primary driver of immediate managerial decision-making: for instance, at a particular time corporate management may be more focused on market share, new market opportunities, or competitive pressures, although in each case these action(s) will be presented as beneficial to future profits. Large (global) corporations frequently seek to shape the political situation in which they find themselves, to further their particular interests, seeking to manage (and influence) public policy debates and decisions that threaten or compromise their strategic goals, and most especially those political developments that might undermine the means by which they are able to reach these strategic goals.[2] If the broad intent behind corporations' actions can be relatively easily inferred in most (although not all) cases, the manner by which their political economic power is deployed is multifaceted and not always easy to clearly pin down. However, the extensive debates about the character of power generally, and the power of corporations specifically, allow a guide to be set out to the range of analytical tools that any investigation of a specific instance might utilize to assess the extent of corporate power.

The power of corporations: in general

The question of power is central to the social sciences and there is a vast literature exploring how it might be analyzed. Rather than rehearse these debates, I will briefly review perhaps the most influential account of the field; Steven Lukes' analysis of the three dimensions of power.[3] Lukes sets out three dimensions that are not (as is sometimes mistakenly assumed) alternatives but make up a rounded and complex account of how social actors attempt to further their interests. Taking each of these dimensions in turn I will briefly set out Lukes' key features and relate these summarily to the corporate political economy before turning to the specifics of how we might analyze the role of corporate power in global governance.

The first dimension (or view) of power focuses on directly observable behavior and decision-making and is perhaps the most frequently deployed account in the media and popular account of corporate politics. Here resources that are deployed to produce results are the primary focus; the more resources an actor has at their disposal the more powerful they will be, and thus the larger the organization or actor the more powerful it is. Focusing on behavior, this approach is usually issue based, examining power in a specific aspect of the political economy where observable conflict has been resolved in favor of a particular actor/agent or group of actors/agents. The interests of the actors concerned are defined through their articulation as a set of policy preferences, and, as such, this is a subjective account of interests relying on those defined and announced by the actors/agents themselves. This approach is often used to measure corporate power by making a comparison between turnover or capitalization and states' GDP, and as I have already argued this approach is misleading. Certainly, corporations offer statements about their reasons for preferring one set of policies over another, justifying their lobbying and influence in the political realm, but it is difficult to assess their power using only a measure of resources. Thus, while this first dimension is a useful component in any evaluation of corporate power it cannot (if we follow Lukes' analysis) be the end of analysis.

In Lukes' account, the first dimension of power is complemented by a second dimension that offers a qualified critique of the first's positive and behavioral focus. Although the importance of resource endowments is retained, the ends to which such resources may be deployed are widened to include the ability to influence and change the decision-making process itself. In the first dimension the decision-making process is taken to be largely given and resources are deployed within it, in the second dimension the process of decision-making is itself impacted by the deployment and use of power resources. Power then is also about the ability to halt or delay decision-making, the ability to keep potential political conflicts out of sight, or to push the moment of decision into some ill-defined future. This allows powerful actors to maintain the status-quo even when other actors/agents might wish to open a public political debate about the issue at hand. Interestingly, this can shade into neglect and lack of support to progress issues; an example might be the lack of corporate interest in further developing the international trade regime (via the currently long stalled Doha round of trade negotiations) as corporations seem to see little further value to be gained from such arrangements, contributing to the inability of the World Trade Organization (WTO) to bring the round to a conclusion. The focus of corporate political interest seems to have moved to regional agreements where specific sectoral or even particular corporations' interests can be better furthered.[4] Here, Lukes' second dimension is manifest through an unwillingness of key (powerful) actors to work towards a specified end.

Conversely, this dimension of power can also be seen operating when issues that seemed (politically) settled are returned to the political realm for re-evaluation. This might be, for instance, when a powerful corporation has a grievance about the manner in which a specific policy has been enacted or in practice impacted their operations. The interests we might identify, however, remain those that are subjectively presented by the actors themselves in their (political) communications, including negative interests, perceptions of market threat or risk. Drawing on first and second dimensional views of power, analysis broadly focuses on behavior, allowing the absence of action to also be regarded as a manifestation of power. However, Lukes argues that while there is much of value that can be discovered and revealed using these two dimensions, they still only offer a partial account, and as such he suggests a third is required to complement the first two.

The third dimension is often referred to as structural power as it suggests the "resources" being deployed are not necessarily physical or material but can be ideational or normative, and as such may not be recognized as "resources" at all in the familiar sense. The key to this approach is the focus on agenda setting. Building on the second dimension's recognition of power in the ability to affect the timing of decision-making processes, it expands the account to include the ability to shape the options around which decisions are made. This most importantly relates to the ability to render certain options as those among which a solution can be chosen and certain other options as nonsensical, inoperable, or invisible. Potential issues are removed from the realm of the possible and kept off the agenda from which decisions may be made. For instance, the almost universal (global) acceptance that corporations should legitimately be treated as legal individuals enjoying a range of rights is not necessarily self-evident, but rather is the result of a political-legislative history. However, it is now regarded as un-contentious, and any argument that might constrain such rights (or even abolish the legal personality of the corporation) is unlikely to reach the realm of "reasonable" political debate. The process by which such agendas are shaped may involve either positive arguments about whether certain proposals are viable or plausible, or can be a radical silence about some potential solutions or approaches to an issue. Most importantly this analysis involves a counterfactual argument that differentiates between subjective (articulated) and real (but unarticulated) interests.

In the first two dimensions of power, to a large extent actors tell us why they act, or it is easy to infer from their general pronouncements what drives their behavior. In the third dimension analysis focuses on the social, political economic context and structure to infer corporations' "real" interests, and to assess what potential factors and issues are being kept out of the political process altogether as they run counter to these interests. This is counterfactual as much that is regarded as shaping the structures of power is unarticulated (and indeed even may be denied) by the actors or agents (the corporations) themselves. In this dimension, it is the ability of corporations to normalize specific ways of shaping political economic affairs (through what is sometimes referred to as the *neo-liberalization* of society) without seeming to have acted which becomes the focus of attention: the normalization of the corporate economy. For some commentators this reflects the emergent power of a transnational capital class seeking to (re)make the global political economy into a neo-liberal market system.[5] So for instance, as Colin Crouch has observed "one of the main achievements of the neo-liberal political project is to place more or less all institutions in society—universities, hospitals, charities as well as governments—under an obligation to behave as though they were business corporations."[6] The ability to set the terms of debates and policy parameters in this analysis reveals the extent of the structural power of (in this case) corporations. Where latent conflicts are identified that we might expect to be socially evident and are hidden or kept off the political agenda, structural analyses see the hand and work of power. However, as Lukes makes clear, like the other two dimensions, a purely/exclusively structural approach to (corporate) power also is incomplete. It is only by according space in our analyses to all three dimensions that we can appreciate the workings of power in the global political economy.

Taking this general approach and applying it more specifically to the global corporate political economy, analyses need to focus on three complementary realms, each of which presents a context in which global corporate power is articulated: as already discussed one common approach focuses on the resources (material and political) that corporations are able to deploy to influence policy makers and other political actors; from the other direction we might also examine the institutional context in which corporations operate, understanding the (relative) political power of corporations by seeing in what manner the cultures, laws, and history in which corporations are embedded shape and influence how corporations seek to further their interests, and how this influences their successful pursuit of their interests; and, thirdly, we can adopt a closer focus on the political environment itself, most specifically the forms of regulation and the political system itself as having significant impact on the manner in which corporations' power is both recognized and understood.[7] Across all of these realms of power and influence, each corporation or group may undertake proactive articulation of its power (deploying its various resources and their perceived "weight"), may merely remain reactive to external prompts (political economic or technical), or if we include the third dimensional analysis of power, may be working to shift and change the agenda of policy and other political debates about the corporate political economy (in ways that may not be immediately obvious). Corporate power then is likely to be multidimensional and enacted across a range of political economic contexts, and as such it now makes some sense to (re)focus on the subject of this book.

The power of corporations: the case of global governance

Complementing the more general analyses of (corporate) power above, Doris Fuchs has suggested that the power of corporations in global governance can be disaggregated into three elements: instrumental power—encompassing direct influence; structural power—revolving around rule-making in global governance which is more indirect, with corporate influence often mediated through national governments; and discursive power—linked to the manner in which certain settlements are politically legitimated outside the formal processes of policy adoption.[8] Fuchs' approach emphasizes Lukes' third dimension by disaggregating structural power into two elements (rule-making power and discursive power), while taking Lukes' first two dimensions as being aspects of instrumental power and collapsing them into one element, although Fuchs' structural power might also be said to sit somewhere between Lukes' second and third dimensions. As this suggests, Fuchs' approach adds some specifics to our assessment of the power of global corporations to influence and shape the structures and practices of global governance.

Starting with instrumental power, Fuchs argues that a major element of this power in the global realm is linked to the various forms of lobbying undertaken by (global) corporations and their associated interest groups. Large corporations are able to both mobilize significant resources to support supranational lobbying work, but also to use their existing networks (within and outside the corporation itself) to reinforce other networks to make such political work more effective.[9] Many, if not all of the international governmental organizations (IGOs) that form the structure of global governance are exposed to (and indeed often welcome) interactions with individual corporations and various lobbying organizations. It is more difficult to place easily in this account those organizations that lie between business groups and official IGOs; a key example of this hybrid is the Transatlantic Business Dialogue (TABD) which was founded in 1995 as a partnership between the US Ministry of Commerce, the European Commission, and the European Roundtable of Industrialists. The group self-avowedly brings together corporations' senior managers, international civil servants, and senior politicians to provide "unfiltered business advice from CEOs, with the objective to work with policymakers in thinking through how best to sustain the dynamism and global impact of the transatlantic economy."[10] Groups like this have often been identified by critics as being the route by which corporations are able to further their interests through direct access to policy makers while side-stepping the operation of national democracies. However, supporters counter that national forums are much too narrowly focused to explore the global market related issues that groups like TABD are formed to address.

That said, given the complexity of global governance and its associated negotiations, it is not clear that even very well resourced corporate lobbying activities necessarily have a direct impact.[11] Certainly, corporations (and their associated interest groups) often are able to outspend civil society groups seeking to reach the same policy makers, and global corporate structures may better map onto global governance networks, but politicians even if friendly to the corporate agenda may (especially in Europe) need to be also sensitive to other groups and interests that are able to articulate their demands through national political systems. Moreover it is not the case that all groups representing corporations are always on the same side of the debate, as it is a mistake to assume that all business related lobbying groups and individual corporations agree about the potential direction of policy or legislation in any specific case. Indeed, it is not unusual in areas of international economic regulation to see representatives from different sectors (differently impacted by the proposed changes in rules or practices) lining up against each other seeking to establish that their position is the *real* interest of business. Furthermore, the fragmentation of party politics across much of the developed world has led to the rise of populist and oppositional parties who are frequently less enamored of the corporate sector than the established parties on the right and left that previously monopolized democratic politics in Europe, America, and beyond.[12] Therefore, corporations and their representatives often favor technocratic governments committed to sound finances and economic policy, as happened during the post-2008 global economic crisis.

Furthermore, Fuchs is careful to stress non-instrumental analyses because only focusing on such direct influence—shifting specific policy deliberations towards particular preferences of certain corporations and groups—misses the aspects of corporate power that inform the "mood music" of global governance.[13] One of the chief structural elements that Fuchs discusses is the relative mobility of (financial) capital, which gives corporations a potential freedom of (re)location seldom enjoyed by other social actors and perhaps more importantly allows them to define such mobility as "normal."[14] Moreover the utilization and employment of those with experience of the corporate sector in the institutions of global governance is likely also to have some effect on how these organizations perceive corporate interests; the networks that stretch between the corporate sector (including the large business consultancies like McKinsey) and global regulatory organizations help normalize the language and priorities of the corporate sector.[15] This "enrolment" of networks into the corporate project suggests that the power and/or influence of the global corporate sector is (partly) achieved by intensifying inter-network linkages to orchestrate the repetition and expansion of preferred narratives and policy prescriptions furthering their normalization, and partial de-politicization.[16]

Moreover, a recent study of the concentration of ownership of global corporations suggests that in 2007 around 80 percent of global corporations' operating revenue was controlled by 737 shareholders, of whom 298 were corporations themselves. The largest of these were all financial sector corporations (with Barclays alone controlling four percent of total operating revenue of global corporations via its share-holdings), although this may have changed post-2008, if not in magni-tude certainly as to which banks are prominent "owners." Although this indicates a concentration of effective control over corporate resources that might lead to a clear identification of instrumental power, the more interesting element here is the manner in which this core con-centrated group of owners would be likely to develop converging views on particular issues related to the corporate sector and be able to pro-mulgate them widely and authoritatively. In addition, these core shareholding corporations are also highly represented in various busi-ness organizations and roundtables, again helping to promote a specific set of interests and viewpoints on the governance of the global corpo-rate sector.[17] The power of the global corporate sector is therefore unlikely to be located in a specific place, or with a specific actor (or small group of actors), but rather is the work of a complex and exten-sive network of agents all in their own interests seeking to further and reinforce elements of the agendas that favor (global) corporations.[18]

These avenues of influence are complemented by the global cor-porations' ability to set the rules in commercial sectors: when large (global) corporations produce technical standards or other standar-dized practices (perhaps within their supply chain) in some ways they have become legislators for the global system;[19] indeed in the issue area(s) in which their standard(s) are operable we could say that they have become institutions of global governance themselves, and have in some cases taken on the role of (soft) law enforcement. Fuchs' sees this "quasi-regulation" as clearly reflecting the agenda-setting power of the cor-porate sector.[20] Firstly, it represents the ability of large (global) corporations to shape regulations to their interests while smaller firms often find their compliance costs are higher (acting as a further competitive advantage for the larger corporate actors). Secondly, likewise any dis-tributional effects are skewed towards the corporations who write the rules and hence if power is about the ability to secure benefits and avoid costs, the move to self-regulation reflects the ability of larger cor-porations to mobilize their power to this end. Lastly, the ability to con-struct (and legitimate) these forms of "quasi-regulation" forestalls and undermines public sector (and perhaps more democratically informed) modes of formalized regulation; self-regulation and intra-network private global governance are to some extent defensive moves aimed at reducing the political "need" for formal regulatory intervention.

This agenda setting power often is related to the ability of global corporations to mobilize specialized and technical knowledge that has perceived value for the global system; however, this is not necessarily a fixed resource or one that is sustainable. For instance the previously dominant Windows/Intel set of technical standards ("Wintelism"), while still dominant, has been challenged by the shift to mobile technology, which in turn has enhanced the ability of other actors (such as Google/Android) to shape new technical standards for digital technologies. As this suggests, corporations cannot rely merely on size and resources to maintain their power over such issues, although of course resistance to change is a key lobbying aim for mature corporations that dominate markets, and one which the defense of certain technical standards may be intended to achieve. Moreover, alongside these forms of agenda setting, the increased use of outsourcing and the development of global supply chains has led many corporations to adopt codes of conduct, either developed internally or adopted from external organizations (as discussed in the previous chapter) which can be seen as part of a private or corporate global governance. Much of this aspect of governance has been developed as a form of self-regulation (albeit with an external audit function) and as such reflects the final aspect of Fuchs' discussion of power: discursive power.

The key outcome of the discursive power of business and the corporate sector has been the elevation of the market to the preferred solution to social challenges: the market will deliver better and more efficient solutions than the state. This shift has been developing over many years and the end of the Cold War (and the "triumph" of liberal capitalism) is often identified as a key moment of normative acceleration. Certainly, this expansion of the political reliance on markets has led to some questions about the moral legitimacy of corporations and the business sector more generally, which to some extent has prompted the interest in and activities around corporate social responsibility set out earlier. As corporations have acquired increasing political authority, so they have been required to justify their role(s) more explicitly, which in its turn has further normalized their political authority across the realms of global governance as legitimate interlocutors of politicians, IGOs, and other groups deliberating on the developing forms of governance in the global political economy.[21] Moreover, the ability to frame the policy discussion also then reinforces the other dimensions of power discussed above; once the discussion is one where competitiveness, efficiency, and the centrality of economic growth to policy are the key foci, corporations are able to make a convincing case that they are the (technical) experts on these issues. Certainly, discursive power can be undermined by events: for instance the ability of the financial sector to maintain its role as the legitimate and well-grounded source of expertise on the governance of global financial markets was dealt a serious blow by the 2008 financial crisis, although equally the strength of the sector's discursive power is revealed by its relative recovery once certain corporations had been sacrificed on the altar of political expediency.

Complementing Fuchs' analysis of discursive power and to some extent underlining the resilience of the financial sector's power after the 2008 crisis, one further critical approach takes a wider view as regards the forms of power that have some impact on the shape and practices of contemporary global governance; this approach puts the "new constitutionalism" at the center of developments in the global political economy. Stephen Gill argues that rather than a relatively neutral set of spatial processes, globalization has involved the establishment of a "market civilization" that represents the latest phase of the expansion of a neo-liberal capitalism that finds its origins in the nineteenth century international system, or (domestically) further back with the nascent liberal state that emerged in Britain in the seventeenth century.[22] Although this is a complex process that has a number of important facets, one of its central elements has been the increasing marketization of social relations, and their consolidation through specific legal forms with the intent of consolidating and furthering the rights and privileges of the corporate sector. Gill sees this process of marketization as being furthered and supported by a set of "disciplinary practices," central to which is the use of legal institutions to structure and shape both state and international political forms of regulation and governance.[23] Gill therefore defines this "new constitutionalism" as:

> A macro-political dimension of the process whereby the nature and purpose of the public sphere in the OECD has been redefined in a more globalized and abstract frame of reference ... [It is] the political project of attempting to make transnational liberalism, and if possible liberal democracy, the sole model for future development.[24] [...] It mandates a particular set of state policies geared to maintaining business confidence through the delivery of a consistent and credible climate for investment and thus for the accumulation of capital ... It stresses the rule of law ... [and expands] state activity to provide greater legal and other protections for business.[25]

Emphasizing "market efficiency; discipline and confidence; economic policy credibility and consistency; and limitation[s] on democratic decision-making processes," this new discipline establishes "binding constraints" on fiscal and economic policy.[26] Perhaps most importantly, this "new constitutionalism" seeks to confirm and if necessary confer privileged rights of citizenship on global corporations.

As Gill notes, "traditional notions of constitutionalism are associated with political rights, obligations and freedoms, and procedures that give an institutional form to the state."[27] However, this new constitutionalism rather than focusing on the rights and obligations of a global citizenry as related to some form of globalized governing body (or bodies), is concerned with a much smaller group, global capital and its operating agents, corporations (national, multinational and global). A key aspect of this constitutionalism is to hold separate the political and economic realms for the purposes of (globalized) governance, ensuring that the economic remains uncontaminated by the political. And it is this discourse of non-contamination that business groups are voracious at furthering. At the center of the "new constitutionalism" is the manner in which specific forms of capitalist social relations are normalized through multilateral agreements on the rights of property owners and investors, and the institutionalization in domestic legislation of these rights, for example with intellectual property rights via the trade-related intellectual property rights (TRIPs) agreement and through the activities of the World Intellectual Property Organization, which have both been heavily influenced by corporate actions and interventions.[28] Although requiring the recognition and protection of non-national property, requiring unrestricted access to national markets, and establishing compensation ("damages") for state actions that impede these rights, such benefits are all set out in supposedly neutral, technical, trading, and investment agreements, which are most directly related to corporations' activities. This assumption of technocratic governance rather than political balancing is a constant refrain from corporations and is a key element of their discursive framing of global governance.

The legal codification provided through the various mechanisms of global governance "locks in" specific free market policies, and the agreements Gill focuses on do not merely recognize and codify already existing and politically legitimized rights, but rather are intended to provide and establish rights for global corporations that previously had been incomplete and unevenly enforced (and in some cases rights that previously did not exist in any formal manner). Perhaps most importantly, for Gill, these legal mechanisms are intended to shield global capital from local, popular democracy (threats "from below"), to insulate property rights from either democratic or oligarchic interference.[29] Political choices are masked or cloaked by their presentation as legal requirements, and therefore where Gill's approach is especially useful is in his analysis of globalized legal instruments, presenting them not as the result of domination and political hegemony, but rather as the method by which such hegemony is both established and maintained.

Therefore, the international legal sphere is not the ground on which political disputes and conflicts are settled, but rather is the manner in which powerful (class) interests shape the forms of political economic relations that can be established, the norms of behavior in the global system. Gill's approach recognizes that the more general legal context underpins political economic power and hegemony even as disputes and conflicts play out within the limited field this legal system maps out. If hegemony in Gill's analysis (in parallel to Fuchs' analysis of discursive power) is about the construction of a common sense as uncontroversial (at the very same time that it serves and privileges specific interests), then the "new constitutionalism" is intended to depoliticize certain aspects of global governance while also attempting to limit the reach of regulation to those realms and issues which global corporations favor and value. This structural power is of course contested and incomplete but helpfully (re)emphasizes the need to complement Fuchs' instrumental power and/or Lukes' first two dimensions of power with an analysis that accounts for how the political economy is (partly) constructed by how it is presented by key players and social groups.

However, it would be a mistake to assume that the internal resources and experience of all established global corporations necessarily directly map onto their political power in the same way. Corporations from emerging markets and/or developing countries for instance have had different sorts of recent experience from established European or American based global corporations, and this may well equip them with a range of skills, behaviors, practices, and tacit knowledge that enable them to better deal with institutional environments that are not familiar to their competitors from developed countries. Indeed given their histories of development these corporations may have considerably greater tolerance for informal institutions and be clearer about how best to influence and affect policy makers, legislators, and others in the political arenas of such informally organized systems.[30] Emerging market based corporations, while functioning in global markets are often therefore more focused on South-South trade relations and thus will utilize their resources and influence differently within networks that are quite different to those that exist around developed-state markets. This is to say that not only does the power of global corporations differ because of size, resources, and networked engagement with political elites, it also differs by virtue of their political economic focus and ability to respond to less formalized or even non-formal institutional structures in the societies in which they seek to operate.

Starting to assess the power and influence of corporations in global governance

In the next chapter I present a case study of the global governance of corporate taxation to give an example of how an analysis of the power and influence of global corporations in a specific realm of global governance might play out. However, first I offer a more general overview of the issues relating to the global realm. I briefly discussed the UN Global Compact and some of its precursors in the previous chapter, but did not set out in any great detail why for many commentators and analysts the development of various corporate codes of conduct has had little positive impact on the overall behavior of global corporations. On one level it is obvious why these initiatives have been unable to prompt major shifts in corporate practice; codes of conduct and guidelines remain voluntary, non-binding, and often originate with the very actors (corporations) whose behavior they are (seemingly) intended to modify. To some extent the Global Compact has side-stepped this problem by proposing that it is a mechanism for changing the internal normative commitments of its partners and as such should be seen less as a regulatory instrument and more as a process of socialization into its principles. The very fact that it has proved impossible to mobilize states and others towards the development of some form of *binding* global corporate standards may for some illustrate the success of corporate discursive power in that this direction of travel is presented both as "unworkable" because of issues around forum shopping and/or the mobility of capital, as well as an inefficient constraint on corporations' "right" to manage their own affairs.

One way corporate power has influenced the global political economy is the ascendance of various business issues to the level of human rights (benefiting from the political weight accorded to such rights in general). Thus, increasingly the free movement of corporations around the global political economy (incorporating where they see fit), and the right to enter markets as competitors alongside the protection of corporate property, are all now seen as fundamental rights analogous to human rights (or in some accounts *as* human rights). This would seem to indicate the expansion of a particular (neo-liberal) way of understanding the legitimate interests of corporations.[31] That said, equally if we accept that corporations are legitimate social actors, it is also the case that we would expect them to have certain rights to act or to have interests (and resources) protected as being part of their legitimate requirement to expect to have a relatively fixed and predictable (legal) environment in which to work. Nevertheless, this should not blind us to how the accomplishment of such a view as relatively un-criticized common-sense has been underpinned by corporations' ability to frame discussions of such issues. To make this a little clearer, Stephen Wilks has usefully set out a complex of six interlocking "normative narratives" that form the core of the corporations' discursive power.

The first two narratives Wilks identifies are the desirability and potential universality of the market as a way of organizing socio-economic activity; the free market delivers efficiency and general welfare better and more effectively than alternatives. Secondly, and complementing this narrative is the perhaps more controversial acceptance (or belief) that all economies are operating within a global market. Here the "local" conditions that may influence and/or prompt corporate invest-ment decisions are defined by state borders, the market is global and variations are between states; meaningful comparisons for a global corporation are seldom between different cities or regions in one state, but between the regulatory regimes, market conditions, and resources available within the territory of a specific national economy. These "two norms provide a barely questioned framework within which gov-ernment leaders and economic policy operates." Thus, there is an idealized narrative of free markets and their global reach which sets the context for the consideration of policy, state actions, and the judgment/assessment of corporate actions and options; these common-sense principles (as they have become) form part of the core of neo-liberalism. That said, Wilks also suggests that "[l]ike many Christians, multi-nationals proclaim the gospel [of neo-liberalism] but do not live by it."[32] Thus, as Kevin Farnsworth has argued at some length this narrative fails to accurately describe the relations between corporations and states, an interaction he terms corporate welfare. He argues that much that the state does for corporations is hidden or obscured by a rhetoric of the need to reduce governmental interference with business (the dominant narratives that Wilks is concerned to identify), while states are providing extensive and important legal and practical support to the functioning of the corporate economy, providing welfare services for a transnational capital class.[33]

Wilks' next two (interconnected) narratives again have considerable advantages for the (global) corporation generally, and for specific cor-porations, as they play one state off against another. It has become the *sine qua non* of governmental policy that economic growth is not only a good thing, but will underpin all other welfare, social, and political goals. Almost any social, political, public health, or environmental problem, we are told, will be solved through economic growth.[34] Given that state expenditures are finally dependent on tax receipts, the engine of economic growth must be the private sector, and thus if growth is endorsed as a political goal in this manner, the discursive power of the corporate sector revolves around the ability to identify particular policies (or as regards the issues being discussed here, particular proposals to establish new global governance mechanisms or introduce new international regulations) as being inimical to economic growth. This narrative is allied with (building on the market norm) a further acceptance that states are competing with each other, although (again as market logic would suggest) there is a proliferation of national models for establishing competitiveness. Nevertheless as Wilks suggests, Michael Porter's depiction of competitiveness being facilitated by states but *delivered* by the corporations that are domiciled therein, set out in *The Competitive Advantage of Nations* remains highly influential. This leads to the general proposition that the "task of governments is ... to work in partnership with corporations, to provide a supportive environment and to *persuade* them to locate their value-adding activities in your country."[35] This presents a clear challenge to states around the global governance of corporate affairs, as coordination and common regulatory standards erode the ability of states to compete to attract the corporations required for competitive success in economic growth.

The final pair of norms that Wilks suggests reinforce corporations' discursive power (and are furthered by such power) are concerned with neo-liberal policy prescriptions and the emergent issue of sustainability. Having dealt with the issue of the neo-liberalization of policy prescriptions in my discussion of Gill's notion of "new constitutionalism" (above), here I will merely add that a key aspect of this neo-liberal agenda has been the construction of a market in corporate ownership which has led to a formalized focus on maximizing shareholder value as the legitimate end for corporate decision-making while also normalizing the putative privileging of shareholder rights and interests (even in reality these are often compromised by the self-interest of corporate managers).[36] The sixth discourse, that of "sustainability," Wilks suggests has been hijacked by the corporate sector and repurposed into "sustainable development," "sustainable growth," and even "sustainable consumerism" all of which allow corporations to develop further the environmental aspects of the claims to be adopting the measure and practices of corporate social responsibility.[37] Corporations have sustainability departments and divisions, celebrate their ability in many cases to offer "sustainable" technologies and/or services, having side-stepped the threat of "conservation" of resources and provided the solution of their sustainable utilization and deployment.

The interaction and cross-fertilization of these norms underpins the light global governance of corporations by engendering a sense that corporations are already accountable to the market (and thereby to their consumers) and are already exposed to the influence of other independent actors such as pressure groups and the news media. This is further reinforced by the development of corporate social responsibility as a further voluntary response to criticisms and which we have already discussed. The discursive power of the global corporate sector has been used to build a governance context in which there is almost a complete lack of formal accountability, while offering many and well-developed opportunities for critics to articulate their concerns, and seek to influence corporate behavior. The question whether such discursive power is legitimate or not depends on the evaluation of the social place, legitimacy, and value of global corporations. Indeed, one might well accept that their discursive power has been able to shape agendas in a socially valuable way in some policy arenas (where one's political economic views are parallel to those of corporations) while criticizing other areas where the direction of travel encouraged by the corporate framing of issues diverges from one's own view of the (global) good life. Like all power, identifying its operations and recognizing its influence does not automatically produce a judgment as regards its acceptability or legitimacy; that is a judgment for the individual analyst.

Conclusion

Finally, and following Wilks, it does not seem unreasonable to regard global corporations as institutions of global governance.[38] Global corporations set standards and rules in many market sectors partly through structural and discursive power, but also because many global sectors actually function as effective oligopolies,[39] and as such are controlled by a small group of corporations whose managers even if not colluding with each other, share the broad norms that Wilks has identified. Moreover, within these networks corporations construct regimes of private law to govern the relations between them, while also seeking to influence public law institutions; private law can be manifest through standard setting as well as through contract law more generally. Thus as Dan Danielsen has pointed out:

> the decisions and actions of corporations have social consequences largely indistinguishable from those created by public regulators, but ... corporate decision-making [i]s largely insulated from public

participation, engagement or scrutiny … If corporations are significant institutions in the transnational governance regime, then policymakers and activists will need to find ways to affect the decision-making of these corporate institutions.[40]

The democratic deficit often identified as compromising the legitimacy of global governance, is repeated and is perhaps more serious where corporations by their very actions are regulating economic interactions, even if these are also shaped by various other regulatory regimes and to a large extent internal to contracted networks across their global supply chains. The choice between competing standards, differential corporate governance regimes, and the incorporation of national rules into standard corporate practices, allow corporations to decide which regimes they might use, how they interpret them, and if, as is sometimes the case, in the face of no acceptable standards or rules they need to set their own for their network's internal interactivity.

Certainly, business groups, of which the International Chamber of Commerce is perhaps most active, seek to harmonize these regimes, while also seeking to shape the manner in which they are mediated into national legal systems,[41] but they also (utilizing the narratives Wilks identifies) try to ensure corporations have significant room to maneuver. Corporations and business associations seek to influence national laws directly via lobbying, but this also plays out in how corporations' lawyers are able to influence how particular laws are interpreted in court hearings. Claire Cutler is not alone in discussing the result of these activities under the rubric of "hard corporate right versus soft corporate responsibilities"; for instance (again) compare the robust rights extended to (mostly) corporate property under the WTO's TRIPs agreement and the guidelines or principles that form part of the UN Global Compact discussed earlier.[42] This lack of symmetry is not an accident or the mere result of happenstance, but rather reveals the operation of global corporate power in its varied dimensions. Thus, in their role as institutions of global governance, global corporations have been able to influence the shape of the regulatory regimes under which they operate, sometimes through indirect means of lobbying or influencing the development of institutional policy and sometime more directly by establishing their own authority to structure and govern specific issue areas. This is to say, corporations are at the same time a focus of attention for institutions of global governance as well as also being such institutions themselves in certain realms of the global political economy.

Indeed, corporate power is often most obvious where the relationship between non-legal regulatory schemes, private law and public
state-based law (global governance) are called into question by other
actors, be they political pressure groups, democratic parties, or other
corporate interests. The ability (or sometimes inability) to develop a
legitimate response to socio-political challenges is when most people
become aware of the salience of corporations' political role. Thus, to
develop some of the themes from this discussion in more detail, in the
next chapter we move to the case of the taxation of corporations,
which represents an interesting case of the interaction between corporate interests and global governance and how corporate power has
sought to shape the field of (non)activity.

Notes

1 Mark J. Roe, *Political Determinants of Corporate Governance: Political Context, Corporate Impact* (Oxford: Oxford University Press, 2003), 203–204.
2 Thomas Lawton, Steven McGuire, and Tazeeb Rajwani, "Corporate Political Activity: A Literature Review and Research Agenda," *International Journal of Management Reviews* 15, no. 1 (2013), 88.
3 Steven Lukes, *Power: A radical view* (second edition) (Basingstoke: Palgrave Macmillan, 2005).
4 Steve McGuire, "Multinationals and NGOs amid a changing balance of power," *International Affairs* 89, no. 3 (2013): 695–710.
5 See: William K. Carroll, *The Making of a Transnational Capital Class: Corporate Power in the 21st Century* (London: Zed Books, 2010); Leslie Sklair, *The Transnational Capital Class* (Oxford: Blackwells Publishers, 2000).
6 Colin Crouch, *The Strange Non-Death of Neoliberalism* (Cambridge: Polity Press, 2011), 167.
7 Lawton, McGuire, and Rajwani, "Corporate Political Activity," 89–96.
8 Doris Fuchs, *Business Power in Global Governance* (Boulder, Colo.: Lynne Rienner Publishers, 2007), 56–58.
9 Ibid., 84–85; Michael Moran, *Business, Politics and Society: An Anglo-American Comparison* (Oxford: Oxford University Press, 2009), 77–82.
10 See the pages of Transatlantic Business Council that hosts the group— http://transatlanticbusiness.org/tabd/–from where this quote is taken.
11 Fuchs, *Business Power in Global Governance*, 93.
12 Moran, *Business, Politics and Society*, 157.
13 My term not Fuchs'.
14 Fuchs, *Business Power in Global Governance*, 108–109.
15 Moran, *Business, Politics and Society*, 80.
16 Heather McKeen-Edwards and Tony Porter, *Transnational Financial Associations and the Governance of Global Finance: Assembling wealth and power* (Abingdon: Routledge, 2013), 31–33.
17 Hugh Compston, "The Network of Global Corporate Control: Implications for Public Policy" *Business and Politics* 15, no. 3 (2013): 357–379.

18 For the extent of these networks and a guide to the shape and character see William K. Carroll and Jean Phillipe Sapinski, "The Global Corporate Elite and the Transnational Policy-Planning Network 1996–2006: A Structural Analysis," *International Sociology* 25, no. 4 (2010): 501–538.
19 Crouch, *The Strange Non-Death of Neoliberalism*, 133.
20 Fuchs, *Business Power in Global Governance*, 132.
21 Ibid., 146.
22 Stephen Gill, "New Constitutionalism, Democratization and Global Political Economy," *Pacifica Review* 10, no. 1 (February 1998): 27–29; Stephen Gill, *Power and Resistance in the New World Order* (Basingstoke: Palgrave Macmillan, 2003), 118.
23 Ibid., 130.
24 Ibid., 131/132.
25 Gill, "New Constitutionalism, Democratization and Global Political Economy," 38.
26 Gill, *Power and Resistance in the New World Order*, 132.
27 Ibid.
28 Christopher May, "Direct and Indirect Influence at the World Intellectual Property Organization" in *Business and Global Governance*, ed. M. Ougaard and A. Leander (London: Routledge, 2010): 39–56.
29 Gill, "New Constitutionalism, Democratization and Global Political Economy," 25, 30.
30 Ali Taleb, "Emerging Multinationals from Developing Countries," in *The Multinational Enterprise in Developing Countries: Local versus global logic*, ed. R. Molz, C. Raţiu, and A. Taleb (Abingdon: Routledge, 2010), 194–207.
31 Danny Nichol, "Business Rights as Human Rights" in *The Legal Protection of Human Rights: Sceptical Essays*, ed. T. Campbell, K.D. Ewing, and A. Tomkins (Oxford: Oxford University Press, 2011), 229–243.
32 Stephen Wilks, *The Political Power of the Business Corporation* (Cheltenham: Edward Elgar, 2013), 164.
33 Kevin Farnsworth, *Social Versus Corporate Welfare: Competing Needs and Interests within the Welfare State* (Basingstoke: Palgrave Macmillan, 2012); see also Joseph E. Stiglitz, "America's Socialism for the Rich," *The Economists' Voice* (June 2009): 1–3, which refers to these sorts of arrangements as "socialism for the rich."
34 Wilks, *The Political Power of the Business Corporation*, 165.
35 Ibid., 165, emphasis added.
36 Laura Horn, *Regulating Corporate Governance in the EU: Towards a Marketization of Corporate Control* (Basingstoke: Palgrave Macmillan, 2012).
37 Wilks, *The Political Power of the Business Corporation*, 167. See for instance the *Financial Times*/UN Global Compact report, *The African Sustainability Barometer*, www.unglobalcompact.org/resources/461.
38 Wilks, *The Political Power of the Business Corporation*, Chapter 7.
39 Jeff Harrod, "The Century of the Corporation" in *Global Corporate Power* (IPE Yearbook 15), ed. C. May (Boulder, Colo.: Lynne Rienner Publishers, 2006), 25.
40 Dan Danielson, "How Corporations Govern: Taking Corporate Power Seriously in Transnational Regulation and Governance," *Harvard International Law Journal* 46, no. 2 (Summer 2005): 424.

41 Gregory C. Shafer, "How Business Shapes Law: A Socio-Legal Framework" *Connecticut Law Review* 42, no. 1 (November 2009): 147–183.
42 Claire Cutler, "Legal Pluralism as the 'Common Sense' of Transnational Capitalism," *Oñati Socio-Legal Series* 3, no. 4 (2013): 719–740; Christopher May, "The Corruption of the Public Interest: Intellectual Property and the Corporation as a Rights Holding 'Citizen'" in *The Challenges of Global Business Authority: Democratic Renewal, Stalemate, or Decay*, ed. T. Porter and K. Ronit (Albany, NY: State University of New York Press, 2010), 179–201.

5 Global governance, corporations and tax

- Taxing global corporations: a (very) short history
- The global governance of corporate taxation
- Tax planning and the reduction of tax
- Apple, non-residence, and tax reduction
- Conclusion

So far I have explored various elements of the interaction between global corporations and global governance, and now I bring these discussions together to explore why, whether, and how global corporations can be taxed. Especially since 2008 and the arrival of the contemporary politics of austerity, the issue of global corporate taxation has risen up the agenda of national and international politics. The business sector seems to have benefited from considerable support in the crisis, but a series of media stories about corporate "tax planning" have indicated that large (often global) corporations have managed to minimize their tax exposure. The question of taxation illustrates many of the issues I have been exploring, and is also particularly timely.

The case for the taxation of business entities and corporations in particular, is most often premised on the benefits that they receive from the state, either directly or indirectly. The direct benefits, as we have seen earlier are concerned with the legal advantages of incorporation and the recognition of corporate legal personality; we might add the recognition of property rights (especially such intangible properties as patents and/or trademarks for instance), and the basic education/training of the workforce. Less direct, but no less significant benefits might include the provision of a stable market economy, ranging from the control/governance of money, through to regulatory issues around contract or labor laws and even more generally the provision of a stable and orderly society. As US Senator Elizabeth Warren put it:

You built a factory out there? Good for you. But I want to be clear: you moved your goods to market on the roads the rest of us paid for. You hired workers the rest of us paid to educate. You were safe in your factory because of police forces and fire forces the rest of us paid for. You didn't have to worry that marauding bands would come and seize your factory ... Now look, you built the factory and it turned into something terrific or a great idea? God bless. Keep a big hunk of it. But part of the underlying social contract is you take a hunk of that and pay forward for the next kid who comes along.[1]

So, a popular position is that as corporations benefit from all these collective goods when they trade and organize their commercial affairs, they might also have an obligation to contribute some of their surpluses to states' budgets to continue the support for the stability of the market system within which they act. Without the state's role in supplying these collective public goods, it would be considerably more costly (if possible at all) for corporations to function, and thus a portion of their profits must stem from not having to organize these collective goods themselves.

This might be regarded as a social contract approach to corporate taxation (indeed Senator Warren uses the term), although one's view of corporate taxation might relate to which society is focused on, the domestic or the global.[2] However, as this chapter will develop, the contemporary logic of corporate taxation is based almost entirely on national jurisdictions, and thus calls for fair and just taxation, which while potentially having a global sensibility, has mostly remained focused on the tax systems in particular countries. Increasingly there seems a public perception that there is a putative "fair" level of taxes one might expect corporations to pay, which in recent popular commentary on corporate taxation has begun to distinguish between the letter and the spirit of the law;[3] certainly "tax planning" can reduce the tax exposure of global corporations, but if corporations wish to be seen as socially responsible, is following the letter of the law enough? Thus, quite apart from the legal issues, now corporate tax seems to also include a political issue around social reputation, as indicated by Starbucks' "voluntary" payment of corporation tax (by foregoing potential allowances) after a public outcry.[4] In other words, for global corporations alongside the legal issues, taxation is becoming part of brand management.

In the most general terms tax has two primary and general functions: firstly, it allocates a society's resources between an authority empowered to collect taxes, through a collective decision-making procedure, and private individuals who have accumulated the resources in the first place. Taxation is how the state gathers together resources to solve collective action problems. Secondly, taxation plays a central role in deter-mining how the social product is divided up between the various actors and groups of actors who make up such a society.[5] In the global political econ-omy the former is decentralized as these decisions remain for the most part to be taken by states; in the latter, given that much of the global divi-sion of social product takes place through corporations themselves, as well as states and intergovernmental institutions, corporate taxation decisions have an effect on a state's available funds for disbursement to any programs of international redistribution, in addition to any effect produced by the international organization of corporate activity.

Political authorities have three key tax problems to resolve: jurisdiction— who has the right to tax; allocation—which activity should be subject to taxation, and what are the appropriate rates; and valuation—how can revenues, expenses, and assets be assessed/priced to calculate tax owed. These issues are compounded at the level of the global economy: global corporations are active across many jurisdictions making the decision about who has the right to tax specific activity far from self-evident; global corporations may effectively share overheads and resources across divisions making the allocation of costs/revenues to particular taxation jurisdictions hardly clear cut. Indeed, corporations quite plausibly argue that for internal overheads and resources they are best equipped to assess and allocate a value, not the tax authorities.[6] And valuing corporate assets (especially if these resources are intangi-ble) is by no means straightforward. Given that the maximization of profit is a key strategic aim for any corporation and that tax reduces the effective net profit rate for dispersal to shareholders, it should hardly be surprising that most corporations are interested in (usually legally) reducing their tax burden. The particular situation of globally active corporations offers heightened opportunities to pursue this end, at the same time that national states are seeking (among other things) to capture tax revenue to support their activities. Before exploring how all of this plays out in the contemporary global system, it may be helpful to briefly review the history of corporate taxation to contextualize the question.

Taxing global corporations: a (very) short history

While tax itself has a long history, stretching back to Ancient Egypt, the taxation of commercial profits independently of owners (which is to say corporate taxation), dates only from the years immediately before the First World War. For centuries the activities of merchants and other commercial operators had been taxed at the borders (often paid by others) or as part of personal income, but even after corporations began to be recognized as separate entities, it took some time for tax authorities to identify their profits as a legitimate subject for tax assessment and payment. Corporations only became subject to direct and *separate* taxation in the first decades of the twentieth century in the United Kingdom and United States. Until then they had been treated merely as collectives of individual shareholders each of which handled their own tax affairs. This position changed in the United States in 1909 when to hold off more radical proposals, a new corporate income tax was introduced and in the United Kingdom during the First World War, when a temporary tax on profiteering (profits above pre-war levels) was imposed, leading to the post-war adoption of the first corporation tax.[7] However, it was not so much the imposition of taxes on corporate profits itself that most caused concern among business leaders it was the emerging possibility of "double taxation" where international businesses were taxed more than once on a specific set of earnings if they operated in a number of tax jurisdictions all of which were developing corporate taxation policies.

Given that the United Kingdom was the world's leading exporter of capital in the period immediately prior to 1914, it is perhaps unsurprising that the question of double taxation was first raised here.[8] While the UK Treasury was prepared to be flexible both during and after the war, by 1920 their view was that this was the sort of issue that should be resolved at the recently formed League of Nations. Between the wars, the League's Fiscal Committee developed an approach that distinguished "active income," which should be taxed at the site of activity, from "passive income," including royalties, dividends fees, and similar, which would be taxed where the main location or head-quarters of the corporation was (still referred to as the "permanent establishment" of the corporation).[9] International regulation through guidelines preserved the sovereign rights of countries to tax while providing some basic if still relatively narrow coordination, and was simple enough to offer the chance of successful negotiation between growing numbers of states. Governments might still disagree about which income sat in which designation, but there was at least a basis for the arbitration of such disputes. During this period, the changing character (and extent) of national taxation also began to encourage both wealthy individuals *and* corporations to find low tax jurisdictions. During the interwar years, the Channel Islands, the Bahamas, and Panama developed services that offered tax residence, financial privacy, and tax advice in response;[10] as governments expanded their tax collection activities, so wealthy individuals and corporations looked for ways of hiding their income.

The coordination of the apportioning of income to tax jurisdiction remained the limit of the (light) international regulation of corporate taxation until after the Second World War, not least as international trade had been at relatively low levels until the post-war recovery; it was not until the 1950s that the web of bilateral tax treaties that continues into the present started to be developed to any great extent. However, quite quickly, the development of bilateral treaties became significant enough for the Organisation for Economic Co-operation and Development (OECD) to codify the emerging consensus on how these agreements should be structured into the Draft Convention on Double Taxation of Income and Capital (1963) which established the principles set out in the next section including those on the assessment of transfer pricing.[11] If tax authorities disagreed on how to assess transfer prices and how these related to tax, there remained a possibility of double taxation, but this was reduced through the inclusion in bilateral treaties of clear guidelines for the arbitration between states over these assessments. In the 1980s, the United States attempted to move the consideration of transfer prices away from the arm's length method (see below), but this was presented in international forums as a unilateral challenge to an existing (and settled) norm, framing global taxation as working to an agreed set of understandings and principles.[12] As proposals to capture more of the potential tax on US corporations' foreign activities were also perceived as a threat to Japanese and European states' tax income, the global corporate sector was able to assemble a considerable resistance to any shifts the United States wished to make during the 1980s.

By 1993, new US regulations no longer included non-arms-length measures, and the OECD guidelines of 1995 further empowered corporate tax payers by encouraging states to accept corporations' own assessment of the transfer price(s) (and other revenues) in the first instance.[13] Most notably, these new arrangements also encouraged states to transfer much of the administrative burden of assessing transfer prices to private sector tax advisors, with the intent of supporting voluntary compliance with guidelines, but with the more obvious impact of supporting "efficient" tax planning (to which we will return). The new millennium saw a continued program of corporate tax reductions, which played out in the reduction of headline rates and in a decline of corporate tax as a share of overall tax receipts (even if absolute amounts were more stable). However, after 2008 the rise of popular anger at the financial sector specifically and the increased political sensitivity of more general corporate issues such as executive pay, has prompted the question of corporate taxation to rise higher up the political agenda than it had been for much of the twentieth century.

The global governance of corporate taxation

If the problem is the effective taxation of global corporations, and global governance is often presented as the appropriate response to *global* issues, then what has been the regulatory response to the claimed shortcomings in taxing global corporations? Unfortunately things remain much as Michael Webb characterized them a decade ago:

> At present, national governments still constitute the key level at which corporate tax governance is located, and some of the most important collective agreements and shared understandings at the international and the global levels reinforce national fiscal sovereignty. There are no elements whatsoever of common tax policies (e.g. harmonization of tax bases and rates); cooperation is limited to managing problems that arise when national jurisdictions overlap, as in the case of double taxation. Use of the term *global tax governance* therefore does not imply that global arrangements are the most important elements of the system—though global influences are becoming more important—nor does it imply that all parts of the globe are included on an equal basis.[14]

The global governance of corporate taxation is limited to guidelines for and coordination of national tax policies. Therefore, what is of interest, given the earlier discussion of global corporate power, is whether this situation is maintained by the operation of such power.

For the most part the contemporary (global) governance of corporate taxation is achieved via bilateral tax treaties, which in many cases reflect the guidelines from the OECD and the United Nations. The global governance of corporate taxation therefore currently combines bilateral legal arrangements with a considerable consensus around methods and practices of national tax collection.[15] Nested within this normative context is an international transfer pricing regime which seeks to constrain the manipulation of transfer pricing for tax advantage by including (and coordinating) transfer pricing regulations as part of national corporate tax codes. The OECD's influential guidelines set out a number of relatively well accepted principles by which corporations should be taxed:

- separate entity: there needs to be an established organizational structure of some sort (be it a division or affiliate) within the state's jurisdiction;
- the source principle: the tax authority has the right to tax all income and assets of this entity earned or received within the country up to its "water's edge" or territorial limits;
- the residence principle: the tax authority stipulates what it would regard as indicating a corporation is resident and then taxes the consolidated profits (after allowed expenses);
- no double taxation: profits should only be taxed once and thus under the OECD's principles the source country is expected to have "first crack" at taxing profits, and the residence country's tax authorities usually do not seek to tax income from foreign affiliates where it has already been subject to a tax assessment in the source country.[16]

The calculation of the profits that might be subject to these principles is, of course, affected by the operation of transfer pricing; the price(s) allocated to intra-corporation and/or intra-network transfers of resources, capital, or services (within a global supply chain).

The manipulation of transfer prices is seen as one of the key mechanisms by which global corporations seek to reduce their tax exposure, and thus tax authorities are keen to establish a common standard for these calculations to reduce such manipulation. The key to attempts at standardization is the "arm's length price"—the price that two *unrelated* entities would set for the transaction if they were carrying out such a transaction in broadly similar circumstances. There are two main ways this price might be calculated: if the corporation also supplies the goods or services to external buyers then that should be the price used for the calculation of internal exchanges/transfers as well; alternatively where there are comparable market exchanges that can be identified between two corporations unconnected to the subject of the tax calculation, this price can be used as a proxy.[17] While this seems to establish a clear guide to how such prices might be legitimately calculated, and is accepted by OECD members as part of its Model Double Taxation Convention,[18] it crucially depends on the issue of comparability. This is complicated by the question of whether activities are *actually* comparable, but it is also subject to two approaches which may produce differing results: a focus on comparable transactions; and a comparison of normal or average profit rates for such transactions to identify outlying pricing indicating manipulation.[19] The latter approach, however, has been subject to considerable criticism by the International Chamber of Commerce's Commission on Taxation in the past, which has argued that the arm's length remains the best and clearest method, not least as in practice they arrive at relatively similar amounts, although arm's length is much less financially intrusive.[20] Indeed, such convergence might suggest that the manipulation of transfer prices is not as evident as many critics suggest.

Leaving aside the difficulties of calculating what revenue might be subject to a tax assessment, there are two further key difficulties with the extensive system of bilateral tax treaties (numbering over 3000 in 2015). Firstly, often ministries of finance see these treaties not as a manner of ensuring fair or equitable corporate taxation, but rather as attractors of foreign direct investment. Secondly, and perhaps more serious for reform of the system, the large number of individual bilateral treaties makes any general shift from the now established principles extremely difficult to accomplish. This is especially problematic as the guidelines (and hence treaties) were designed for an age when portfolio investment— the purchase of shares in *existing* foreign entities—was the dominant form of internationalization, whereas in the last half-century the dominant mode of investment has shifted to foreign direct investment (FDI). Coupled with the extensive discretion that corporations have over their preferred financial and organizational structures, the move to FDI has further reduced the ability of states' governments to easily access data on prices as they are now almost completely internalized within the corporate network/supply chain.[21]

However, for global corporations, double taxation remains a significant issue; there is always the possibility that because of the manner in which different tax jurisdictions measure and assess the profits liable for taxation, certain earnings may be taxed twice. To deal with this "danger," most capital exporting countries now have well developed measures in place to alleviate this problem: these may be either unilateral (irrespective of any reciprocal relief from other states) or based on bilateral agreements. In both, this is achieved through either tax credits or by tax exemptions: in the former any tax paid in the source state is credited against an assessment of the global profits by the residence state, meaning that profits are all taxed at the prevailing rate in the country of residence (but only once); in the latter, where tax has been paid on profits in a source state, such profits are exempted from tax in the residence state.[22] As is clear, in the latter case where tax exemptions are used, there is considerable potential for the reduction of taxes through transfer pricing, but as the exemption method is considerably easier for tax authorities to administer it is often the preferred method of avoiding the double taxation of global corporations.

Tax planning and the reduction of tax

Two of the abiding narratives that have been fostered by corporations, (discussed in the last chapter) and which underpin their power, involve the recognition of the existence of a global market alongside the acceptance that states compete against each other. These have clear consequences in the area of the global taxation of corporate activity and profits. Although taxation issues are usually accorded relatively low importance in business surveys, and rhetoric aside, corporations seldom treat taxation as primarily a "locational tournament" in the immediacy of an investment decision, nevertheless the consideration of tax regimes does play a contributory role in longer-term considerations about the location of corporate activity and resources, *alongside* other social, political, and economic issues.[23] It is therefore unsurprising that a recent comparative study of European states confirmed that the chief driver behind the reduction in statutory corporate tax rates in the EU has been the competition between states for corporate activity.[24] This competition can be conducted through headline rates of corporate taxation, or perhaps more effectively (for the policy ends it is meant to support) via preferential tax treatment for particular activities or sectors. The wide range of tax rates, allowances, and preferential treatment gives significant scope for global corporations to utilize their structure and supply chains to reduce their tax exposure. Moreover, unlike other areas of EU policy where policy effects are initially obscure, the costs to the member states of coordination are more immediately visible as it would remove a key perceived policy lever for encouraging corporate investment. As such, coordination (as opposed to competition) has lacked the political support other areas of economic coordination have garnered.

This tax competition is compounded by the problem of transfer pricing, or more accurately the *manipulation* of transfer pricing. However, it is not easy to assess the extent of transfer-pricing manipulation and abuse in the global system; while there are some empirical studies, these are highly selective as they are often focused on specific sectors, or emerge as the result of other investigations into corporate misconduct. Indeed, International Accounting Standards Board guidelines require consolidated accounts, with only relatively relaxed standards on segmental disclosure that make unpicking the location of activity, the logic of transfer payments and the likely effective reductions in tax difficult to ascertain.[25] However, most developed states now have transfer pricing monitoring units and have legislated for powers to reallocate profits when misallocation has been identified.[26] This may indicate that states' governments at least believe without clear deterrence the temptation to manipulate transfer prices would be too great, and would result in significant tax losses.

Transfer prices can be manipulated by *increasing* the charge for a product or service made by a corporate division or affiliate in country A when it is moved or provided to an associated corporate division or affiliate in country B; any surplus/profit on activity is reduced in country B and essentially transferred to country A by the corporation's internal account of its revenue flows; this then changes the tax exposure in both countries. In country B the tax exposure is reduced as costs of the activity have gone up thereby reducing the surplus that could be subject to taxation, while in country A receipts have gone up (against a stable cost base) and thus there is a higher surplus that may be taxed. Where tax is high in country B and low in A, the corporation's overall tax burden therefore has been reduced leaving more funds for dispersal to shareholders. This effect is not limited to taxes on profits; the manipulation of prices may also have a significant impact (for material goods at least) on the exposure to customs duties for intra-corporate transfers around the supply chain. However, the reduction of tax may not be the only motivation for manipulating transfer pricing: it may also reflect internal incentives to particular divisions, and the need to manage the perception of profitability in particular affiliates for other political reasons, such as labor disputes over the share of profit allocated to wages; it may also be intended to stabilize internal cost transfers for strategic planning reasons.[27] However, the primary reason seems to be tax related, and as such is the subject of considerable attention by those seeking to reform global corporate taxation.

While tax planning (which it should be stressed in most cases does not involve illegal tax evasion) is centered on transfer pricing, it is not limited to the simple model set out briefly above. Tax can be reduced also by shifting the timing of payments (easily achieved from within a global corporation's multi-divisional network), and by re-characterizing the payment, perhaps by raising funds for investment in one country and then charging them to a subsidiary in a high tax jurisdiction at above market rates or by re-profiling profits as fees for the use of the main corporation's intellectual property. However, the key manner in which transfer pricing becomes more complex is through the deployment of intermediary recipients for transfers, often holding companies or trusts domiciled in a low tax jurisdiction. Here between the source and resident countries, one or more conduit locations are introduced, each of which will process fees, income, and other payments in a way that will reduce taxation.[28] Indeed, given the nature of bilateral treaty making for corporate taxation, considerable advantages can be gained by taking advantage of various specific aspects of the treaties; for Sol Picciotto this amounts to "treaty shopping taking advantage of the fictions of legal personality and state jurisdiction."[29] Of course, until the revenues have been returned to the residence state they are in most cases not subject to taxation at all; tax is usually only levied on remitted profits.

This deferral of taxation is intended to offer an incentive to corporations to reinvest their profits in their foreign ventures rather than repatriate them. However, as the profits themselves may be moved around the internal networks of the global corporation, this deferral also means that profits can be "parked" in jurisdictions where they attract no tax whatsoever, so called "tax havens." It is in these havens that the global corporations' intermediary recipients are often located, where re-profiling of revenues and re-allocations can take place; sometimes in a revealing term, these are referred to as a corporation's "fictional residence." Most notably, developed capital exporting countries have done little until relatively recently to try and constrain the role of countries that have set out to become tax havens. While happy to intervene in other states' economic policy in areas from government subsidies, trade barriers, and notably intellectual property rights, substantial moves to try and deal with the tax reducing impact of tax havens have only really gathered pace in the new millennium.[30] This may be because, other than the states themselves, there is no vocal global business constituency arguing for such measures (indeed they are more likely to argue for their right to plan their global tax affairs), and the strong association between state sovereignty and taxation has discouraged states from seeking to intervene in the way they have in other areas.

This changed in the late-1990s following the OECD's report on harmful tax competition, which singled out for criticism the willingness to allow residence for preferential tax treatment where there was no associated substantial economic (or other) activity. The OECD Forum on Harmful Tax Practices, which was formed in the wake of the report, relatively quickly identified 41 jurisdictions that could be regarded as being tax havens of one sort or another.[31] However, while other elements of tax havens' practices became subject to some modification after the turn of the millennium, most obviously a move towards more transparency and the slow development of a readiness to explore the question of information exchange—partly linked to the new focus on terrorist organizations' funding in the wake of the attack on the Twin Towers in New York—the issue of "fictional residence" was left to one side. The tax havens, successfully (once the United States had weighed in on their side) argued that the OECD was not a democratically legitimate body to propose global tax standards, and that while their practices were being targeted, tax-distorting preferential treatment by OECD countries themselves was being ignored; they identified key international norms, most importantly democratic accountability and equality of treatment, that they were able to mobilize to force a political compromise.[32] In addition, the OECD had always had a close relationship with the corporate sector, and as such was influenced not only by explicit lobbying but by a history of collaboration on various aspects of the OECD's work. The OECD's culture of consensus also encouraged the development of positions that appealed to all its stakeholders, and corporate representatives were not in favor (understandably) of reducing their ability to govern their own networks, or plan their exposure to tax.

This approach in itself reinforced the general economic perspective that the OECD adopted in its work, which was to stress the value and contribution of corporations to economic development.[33] The corporate sector was thus able to influence the retreat from the strong position through its internal influence, once its representatives had had time to assess the perceived administrative costs and impact on profitability of the OECD's plans, and also via the US state once its government had been convinced of the detrimental effect the proposed measures would have on US corporations' global profitability.[34] Not all corporations necessarily support the activities of tax havens, although most divide on the basis of scale: the larger and more global the corporation, the more likely it is to take advantage of the forms of tax planning tax havens facilitate, and thus the more likely they were to argue against the OECD measures; more nationally focused corporations were likely to see tax havens offering global corporations unfair (tax-based) advantages.[35] In the end, as Jason Sharman has argued at length, the OECD was caught up in a rhetorical struggle about how to define the issue of tax havens—was it one of state sovereignty, equity in treatment of freedom to tax and technical standards, or was it a political issue of developed countries' attempt to reduce the ability of corporations to play one state off against another, alongside the desire of the OECD member states to develop a standardized regulatory system of taxation? In the end, the tax havens were able to convince global policy elites that the OECD was not in the position of being able to legitimately impose its members' preferred standards on non-members.[36]

The issue of state sovereignty trumped other arguments when it came to corporate taxation, but also has a less obvious effect. If tax planning was completely efficient we might expect to see the effective tax rates paid by global corporations converge on a rate which might allow states to reproduce the public goods required for corporate success, while minimizing any further contribution to (global) society. However, recent data indicate that the residence of a corporation does have some impact on the level of tax it pays, suggesting that the ability to game the competitive global tax system is far from comprehensive. Thus, while there has been a general decline in effective tax rates, the ranking of which states are high tax and which are lower has remained stable, and corporations domiciled in higher tax states (such as Japan or the United States) continue to pay higher levels of tax.[37] Nevertheless this system of competitive tax jurisdictions still effectively leaves the global governance of corporate taxation to the corporations themselves with somewhat predictable results when pushed to the extreme by those corporations whose power resources are the most developed, as the recent case of Apple's tax affairs reveals.

Apple, non-residence, and tax reduction

Apple is not the only corporation to be deploying the tax planning strategies I have briefly discussed, but Apple's case has been particularly noted, not least because of the ubiquity of its technology. This particular tax strategy is sometimes referred to as the "Double Irish" or "Dutch Sandwich" or both. Its key elements include:

- the formation of two companies incorporated in Ireland—but one of which has its "effective center of management" in a tax haven;
- the corporation managed in the tax haven is paid a fee by the company domiciled in Ireland to manage and sub-license the group's intellectual property;
- the company in the tax haven is an Irish company for the purposes of "managing" and calculating transfer prices (utilizing the arrangements in bilateral tax treaties) but is based in the tax haven for Irish taxation purposes, thereby reducing its tax exposure to nil;
- no income is logged in the United States, and none in Ireland as the management fee income balances off against royalty payments to the company in the tax haven; and
- finally, by funneling all payments via another subsidiary in the Netherlands, which has an exemption for payments *within* the EU, all tax exposure is avoided.[38]

Thus, Apple is able to use its extensive intellectual property to transfer its income via license fees to a jurisdiction (in this case Bermuda) which has no corporation tax at all. Tax in the United States where Apple is headquartered is avoided by not repatriating the income (a common practice) and while much of the work is conducted in Ireland, the utilization of Apple's technology patents, designs, and trademarks "require" such substantial fees to be paid to the sub-licensing arm in the tax haven so that there is no profit left to tax.[39] This has led to some accusations that for tax purposes at least, Apple has (like some other corporations using similar methods) established a position where they are effectively resident *nowhere* for tax purposes.

These arrangements have enabled Apple like other companies to divide up their profits (and where they are taken) not by virtue of where the activity is based, but rather by where they choose to pay tax. However, holding large accrued profits abroad can present problems when investment is required in a high(er) tax jurisdiction. Apple has developed two strategies to attempt to deal with this: a policy approach; and a fiscal approach. The former involves a campaign by Apple and other corporations with off-shore profits to have the US government extend a "repatriated profits holiday" to allow these funds to be returned to the United States tax free (instead of being taxed when returned to the home jurisdiction). Of course, this continues the tax planning, as having avoided tax on these profits by keeping them off-shore (delaying repatriation), Apple (and others) now want to avoid even this subsequent "cost" of their strategy.[40] The second strategy is to borrow money in the United States to invest there, thereby avoiding repatriating profits to invest, and also producing a useful tax-allowance against subsequent interest payments. However, in Apple's case this money is actually being used to return money to shareholders by buying back their shares, thereby avoiding any tax on dividends.[41] Indeed, while here Apple raised money externally, other companies (such as Starbucks) use intra-group loans (between different jurisdictions) to achieve similar "tax efficiencies."[42] Pressure on the Irish government particularly has led to a commitment to end the possibility of tax-related statelessness for (Irish domiciled) corporations, but it is unlikely that action in one state will halt the ability of corporations to manage their tax affairs in this manner, even if the particularities change.

As this demonstrates, corporate tax planning is alive and well, largely unaffected by the OECD and others' attempts to make taxation subject to global governance by international governmental organization.[43] However, the attempt to establish a new regime for global corporate taxation has not been entirely unsuccessful. The Financial Action Task Force has managed through accreditation and reputational effects to remove some of the most secretive jurisdictions from the acceptable range of locations for corporations to set up fictional residence, but while the choices have changed the practice of tax planning, utilizing intermediaries and transfer pricing remains a key element of global corporate practice.

Conclusion

What is perhaps most interesting about the global governance of corporate taxation (or lack thereof) is how it differs from other areas of global economic governance. Whatever the micro-differences, states *and* global financial-sector corporations alongside other interested commercial actors all want the same thing—global financial stability—and as such have a shared perception of the likely outcome.[44] When it comes to global corporate taxation, however, there is a clear divergence of interest: corporations, their tax advisors, and their global representative bodies all want to reduce the tax exposure (and payments) of corporations; states, on the other hand, want to maintain or even expand this significant (albeit relatively modest) share of total government revenues, not least as other taxes are more unpopular with voters. When states involve corporations and their supporters in discussions of effective corporate taxation, they introduce a major and influential group whose interests are diametrically opposed to the states themselves. This then allows corporations and their associates to frame the issue of taxation as one which pits states against states, rather than states against corporations.[45] However, since the global economic crisis of 2008 there has been an upswing of non-governmental organizations' interest in the hitherto arcane area of global taxation, making the need to shape the agenda of the possible even more pressing for the global corporate sector.

As Grahame Dowling has discussed, the post-crisis upswing in interest in the morality of tax avoidance has resulted in a link being made with corporate social responsibility (CSR). Indeed, a greater appreciation of the rights and benefits that corporations receive has led to a concern with their ability to maneuver around their (moral?) obligation to contribute to the maintenance of these benefits via taxation. However, the spirit of the law and its actual content (the letter of the law) can often be counter-posed. As Dowling concludes, this offers some difficulty for advocates of CSR as often for the stakeholders, the reduction of tax may enable the corporation to offer them expanded benefits; even if the range of stakeholders is expanded it is not clear whether there can be a legitimate political demand for corporations to go *beyond* their legal obligations, not least of all as there is little agreement about what is the "fair share" of tax that corporations should be paying, nor how one justifies shifts from the current situation, other than via democratic governance.[46] However, in Colin Williams and Álvaro Martinez's recent study of tax morality in Europe, the more developed a member state is (using a measure of gross domestic product per person), and the higher direct taxation *and* governmental social expenditure, the less tolerance there is for tax avoidance.[47] This goes some way to indicating why given the threats to social expenditure under austerity in Europe, perceived corporate tax avoidance has become something of a political rallying point. That said, these debates often end up with demands for changes in the tax laws themselves, and confront the issues raised about states' perceptions of inter-state competition.

Interestingly, Phillip Genschal and his co-authors have demonstrated that intra-EU tax competition has driven corporate taxes down much quicker than in the rest of the world; this has partly been a result of the inability to gain wider agreement on tax coordination leading to a focus only on reducing competition in narrowly targeted preferential tax regimes.[48] Moreover, the European Court of Justice's tax jurisprudence has in their assessment tended "to accord higher priority to the protection of taxpayers' treaty-based rights of mobility than to member states' public policy requirements."[49] Indeed, one might conclude that within the EU, corporations now enjoy a constitutional right to enjoy the fruits of tax jurisdiction shopping, an exercisable option on where they are taxed. Once this is linked to the continued existence of tax havens, it seems clear that for global corporations at least, the range of options available as regards tax planning is related to internal organizational needs and priorities with some (potential) regard for the reputational issues that the sometimes adverse publicity around tax planning may prompt, and is not particularly well linked to the revenue needs of the states in which they operate.

As corporations are able to move their profits to low-tax jurisdictions almost at will, the very competition for foreign direct investment that prompts tax competition is weakened, even as states' governments try to compete to host new global corporate investments.[50] This leaves global corporations to decide on investment (and the expansion of existing commitments) on the basis of the internal priorities, with relatively less requirement to be as concerned about the particularities of the tax regime. Moreover, this shifts the logic of tax collection: developed states especially now often seek to raise revenue from smaller corporations and companies whose capital is far from as mobile as their global competitors, and other factors of production, most obviously labor; again this enhances the competitive advantage of the global corporations in national markets, and this has not gone un-noticed by smaller commercial operators. In less(er) developed countries, while they likewise are affected by the ability of corporations to shift profits, they have less opportunity to widen the tax base in response, and thus have seen their tax revenues shrink while the demands on the state have expanded. This has led to a shift to indirect taxation and, to some extent, expansion of taxes on labor, again causing more difficulties to domestic businesses than their global counterparts not least of all because of the impact on effective demand.[51] Tax planning has, therefore, a significant but uneven impact on states; some are able to replace "lost" corporate tax revenues and others are not. In this sense tax planning can act to further inequalities and uneven development in the global system, at the same time that it seems to work with the grain of the global political economy of sovereign states.[52]

Finally, one rather different way of thinking about tax has been suggested by Liam Murphy and Thomas Nagel who argue that we need to recognize property rights are a convention and as such we should regard "property as what is created by the tax system rather than what is disturbed or encroached by the tax system. Property rights are the rights people have in the resources they *are entitled to control* after tax, not before."[53] This approach is instructive when it comes to the taxes paid by non-natural, corporate persons. Certainly there *may* be an argument for natural individuals that their existence pre-dates the state (and its legal system) and thus tax affairs might be regarded as following occupancy or possession. However, corporations as discussed earlier are entirely creations of the (states') law and as such their entitlement to control resources is dependent on state-instituted incorporation. This then might lead us to think that there could be a direct link between the legitimacy of incorporation and the legitimacy of state taxation. This would shift debates (to slightly modify Murphy and Nagel's description) from:

> not how much of what is [a corporation's] the government should take in taxes, but ... [to] how the laws, including the tax system, should determine what is to count as [is a corporation's] ... [This] would not end disagreements over the merits of redistribution and public provision, but would change their form. The question would become what values we want to uphold and reflect in our collectively enacted system of property rights.[54]

The question of taxation would then be moved from the presumption that corporations have a legitimate right to use whatever methods they are able (within the under-regulated international realm) to reduce taxes, to one that linked their exposure to (levels of) taxation to the clear benefits they are able to enjoy through state-mandated incorporation.

The problem of the global governance of corporate taxation is a question of how the issue itself is framed. If it remains a question of state sovereignty over taxation, then while there may be some moves to shift and change institutional guidelines and global norms, then the terrain on which transfer pricing and global corporate tax planning takes place is unchanged. If the issue is framed as one of tax avoidance, the social responsibility of corporations to fulfill their "fair tax" obligations, then the regime itself at present does not deliver anything other than moral persuasion. The discourses that Wilks has identified are crucial in shaping the manner in which corporations have been able to maintain their freedom to plan their global tax affairs, and ensure that the global governance of global corporate taxation remains at the level of guidance about bi-lateral tax treaties.

Notes

1 Quoted in John Naughton "So the big internet firms are chipping in? About time ...," *The Observer* (section: *The New Review*), 17 August 2014: 21.
2 Thomas Rixen, "Tax Competition and Inequality: The Case for Global Tax Governance," *Global Governance* 17 (2011), 456.
3 Grahame R. Dowling, "The Curious Case of Corporate Tax Avoidance: Is it Socially Irresponsible?" *Journal of Business Ethics* [Online First] (August 2013), http://link.springer.com/article/10.1007/s10551-013-1862-4#page-1.
4 *BBC News website*, "Starbucks pays UK corporation tax for first time since 2009," 23 June 2013 www.bbc.co.uk/news/uk-politics-23019514.
5 Liam Murphy, and Thomas Nagel, *The Myth of Ownership: Taxes and Justice* (Oxford: Oxford University Press, 2002), 76.
6 Lorraine Eden, "Taxes, Transfer Pricing and the Multinational Enterprise" in *The Oxford Handbook of International Business*, ed. A. Rugman (Oxford: Oxford University Press, 2009), 596.
7 Martin Daunton, *Trusting Leviathan: the Politics of Taxation in Britain 1799–1914* (Cambridge: Cambridge University Press, 2001), 211.
8 Sol Picciotto, *Regulating Global Corporate Capitalism: International Corporate Law and Financial Market Regulation* (Cambridge: Cambridge University Press, 2011), 219.
9 Ibid., 220.
10 Ibid., 238.
11 Michael C. Webb, "Shaping International Corporate Taxation" in *Global Corporate Power* (IPE Yearbook 15), ed. C. May (Boulder, Colo.: Lynne Rienner Publishers, 2006), 110.
12 Ibid., 113.
13 Ibid., 115.
14 Ibid., 107.
15 Thomas Rixen, *The Political Economy of International Tax Governance* (Basingstoke: Palgrave Macmillan, 2008), Chapter 5, offers a detailed history of the development of the consensus around the avoidance of double

taxation, which he identifies as being the core consensual value of tax governance in the international system.

16 Lorraine Eden, "Taxes, Transfer Pricing and the Multinational Enterprise" in *The Oxford Handbook of International Business*, ed. A. Rugman (Oxford: Oxford University Press, 2009), 599–600.

17 Ibid., 602.

18 Peter T. Muchlinski, *Multilateral Enterprises and the Law* (second edition) (Oxford: Oxford University Press, 2007), 278.

19 Eden, "Taxes, Transfer Pricing and the Multinational Enterprise," 602–611, goes into considerably more detail on these various methods, but space precludes an extensive treatment here.

20 Muchlinski, *Multilateral Enterprises and the Law*, 287.

21 Picciotto, *Regulating Global Corporate Capitalism*, 224–225.

22 Muchlinski, *Multilateral Enterprises and the Law*, 264–266.

23 John H. Dunning and Sarianna Lundan, *Multinational Enterprises and the Global Economy* (second edition) (Cheltenham: Edward Elgar, 2008), 614–617.

24 Michael Overesch and Johannes Rincke, "What Drives Corporate Tax Rates Down? A Reassessment of Globalization, Tax Competition and Dynamic Adjustment Shocks," *The Scandinavian Journal of Economics* 113, no. 3 (2011): 579–602; see also Phillip Genschel, Achim Kemmerling, and Eric Seils, "Accelerating Downhill: How the EU Shapes Corporate Tax Competition in the Single Market," *Journal of Common Market Studies* 49, no. 3 (2011): 585–606.

25 Muchlinski, *Multilateral Enterprises and the Law*, 361–375.

26 Ibid., 276.

27 Dunning and Lundan, *Multinational Enterprises and the Global Economy*, 622–623.

28 Picciotto, *Regulating Global Corporate Capitalism*, 228–229.

29 Ibid., 230.

30 Webb, "Shaping International Corporate Taxation," 118.

31 Ibid., 119; J.C. Sharman, *Haven in a Storm: The Struggle for Global Tax Regulation* (Ithaca, NY: Cornell University Press, 2006), 40–47.

32 Richard Woodward, "Winning and Losing in the Global Economy: The Case of the OECD's Harmful Tax Competition Initiative," *Centre for Global Political Economy* (Working Paper 04–04) (Burnaby: Simon Fraser University, 2004), 8–9; Sharman, *Haven in a Storm*, Chapter 3.

33 Webb, "Shaping International Corporate Taxation," 120.

34 Woodward, "Winning and Losing in the Global Economy," 12.

35 Sharman, *Haven in a Storm*, 66.

36 Ibid., *passim*.

37 Kevin S. Markle and Douglas A. Shackelford, *Cross Country Comparisons of Corporate Income Taxes*, NBER Working Paper Series No. 16839 (February) (Cambridge, Mass.: National Bureau of Economic Research, 2011).

38 Steven A. Bank, "The Globalization of Corporate Tax Reform," *Pepperdine Law Review* 40 (2013): 1311.

39 See Christopher May, "The Corruption of the Public Interest: Intellectual Property and the Corporation as a Rights Holding 'Citizen'" in *The Challenges of Global Business Authority: Democratic Renewal, Stalemate, or Decay*, ed. T. Porter and K. Ronit (Albany: State University of New York Press, 2010), 179–201, for the more general question of why recognizing

corporations as intellectual property rights holding "citizens" can result in political economic difficulties for states.

40 See: Charles Duhigg and David Kocieniewski "How Apple Sidesteps Billions in Taxes," *New York Times*, April 29 2012. http://www.nytimes.com/2012/04/29/business/apples-tax-strategy-aims-at-low-tax-states-and-nations.html?pagewanted=all&_r=0.

41 See: Sarah Gordon "US Taxpayers not the only losers on Apple's megabond," *Financial Times* (Companies section—Weekend FT), May 4 2013: 14.

42 See: *Financial Times*, "How Starbucks stirs things up to pay no UK tax" (Weekend-Alphaville), December 15 2012: 28.

43 As this book goes to press, two developments are of note: the Irish government has recently undertaken to end its much criticised tax policy which underpinned the "double Irish" tax strategy; and the OECD has proposed to the Group of 20 developed countries a new action plan, based on work by its Base Erosion and Profit Shifting project which is intended to combat tax avoidance by global corporations; it is too early to say whether this will be adopted by G20 and whether any formalized and effective regulatory instruments will emerge from this initiative.

44 Here I leave aside those elements of the financial sector that thrive on volatility and crisis, and of course there are some.

45 Webb, "Shaping International Corporate Taxation," 109, 117.

46 Dowling, "The Curious Case of Corporate Tax Avoidance."

47 Colin C. Williams and Álvaro Martinez, "Explaining cross national variations in tax morality in the European Union: an exploratory analysis," *Studies of Transition States and Societies* 6, no. 1 (2014): 5–18. In 2013 the annual Ipsos Mori poll for the Institute of Business Ethics found that in the UK the issue of corporate tax avoidance and evasion now was the top rated concern of respondents when asked about the ethical behavior of businesses. See: Brian Groom "Tax avoidance replaces bosses' pay at top of concerns about ethics," *Financial Times*, November 28 2013. http://www.ft.com/cms/s/0/ac44e12e-578b-11e3-86d1-00144feabdc0.html#axzz38HCxq35s.

48 Genschal *et al.*, "Accelerating Downhill," 591, 596.

49 Ibid., 600.

50 Rixen, "Tax Competition and Inequality," 451.

51 Ibid., 453; Joshua Aizenman and Yothin Jinjarak, "Globalization and Developing Countries—a Shrinking Tax Base?," *Journal of Development Studies* 45, no. 5 (2009): 653–671.

52 *Spillovers in International Corporate Taxation*, International Monetary Fund Policy Paper (May 9 2014) Washington, DC: IMF. The IMF refers to this as "spillover"; perhaps the most interesting thing about this publication is the fact that the IMF is now concerned about states' ability to raise tax revenues and the impact this has on the effectiveness of economic and fiscal policy.

53 Murphy and Nagel, *The Myth of Ownership*, 175, *emphasis added*; I discuss the conventional approach to property rights at some length in Christopher May, *The Global Political Economy of Intellectual Property Rights: The new enclosures* (second edition) (Abingdon: Routledge, 2010), Chapter 1.

54 Murphy and Nagel, *The Myth of Ownership*, 176.

6   A complex relationship

- **Global corporations as subjects of global governance**
- **Global corporations' influence over global governance**
- **Global corporations as global governance institutions**
- **Conclusion**

In Frederick Pohl and Cyril Kornbluth's well-known dystopian science fiction novel *The Space Merchants*, the world is ruled by corporations with states' primary role supporting these giant companies' needs; global advertising agencies manipulate the population's desires and perceptions while products are contaminated with addictive additives and the workforce is treated as expendable. Environmental degradation and resource scarcity have compromised much of human existence, but the ruling corporate elite thrive and the general population is told they have never had it so good.[1] For many critics of the contemporary global corporate sector, although this is an exaggeration, nevertheless it seems to be the likely endpoint of the journey global society is now on. Here I do not consider whether Pohl and Kornbluth's world is any nearer that it was half a century ago, but I do suggest that we cannot assess the relationship between global corporations and global governance (and thereby a large element of global politics) merely by assuming that global corporations are all-powerful and not subject to any democratic accountability nor limiting political power. Rather, it seems to me, as I hope I have established in this book, the relations between global governance and global corporations are complex and our account of power in this relationship needs to be nuanced and multi-faceted.

Conversely, let me also be clear: I have presented global corporations across three dimensions of interaction with global governance (as reviewed below), and in each dimension global corporations (individually or in groups) have considerable ability to shift and change agendas and outcomes, but this ability is hardly uncontested. Although the political economic power of global corporations is often evident in global governance and there have been times and issues over which this power has expanded, global corporations have also frequently found their influence compromised or countered. There have been (and will continue to be) situations when corporations have been subjected to increased regulation, increased countervailing influence, and have not been able merely to dictate ends. These varying cases require too much detailed analysis for a short book like this, but what I have hoped to do in these chapters is to suggest the analytical terrain over which such judgments and analyses can be developed. Therefore in this conclusion, I briefly review the three main dimensions of the relations between corporations and global governance.

Global corporations as subjects of global governance

The corporation, like most natural individuals,[2] remains unrecognized in international law; its subjects remain predominantly states and their governments. Corporations, despite operating globally, are still *located* in states and thereby like natural persons are exposed to the regulations and constraints set out in global governance via states' jurisdiction over their activity (hence my rejection of the term *transnational* corporation in the Introduction). If we limit our consideration of global governance to formally enforceable legal instruments, however, we also limit our understanding of the manner in which global corporations may be subject to regulatory and other (global) influences over their practices and activity. As a result of the character of the international legal realm and its formally state-related focus, many of the elements of global governance that have sought to shape and regulate global corporations have been advisory, indirect, or effectively voluntary. Although this means that these forms of governance are less enforceable, this should not be taken to mean they are without influence. Therefore, when thinking about the manner in which corporations are exposed to global governance, it is as well to think of this as a spectrum from legal-like instruments at one end to the guidelines and advisories at the other.

At the most robust end of the spectrum of corporate-focused global governance we might place the World Trade Organization (WTO) Trade Related Intellectual Property Rights (TRIPs) agreement, or the complex of bilateral investment treaties (BITs) that have been developed in the last half-century. The TRIPs agreement, while placing considerable obligations on members of the WTO, also constrains and shapes the manner in which corporations can (re)use intellectual property, and has prompted corporations to shape their knowledge management strategies in particular ways.[3] Likewise BITs, while ostensibly concerned with the activities of states and their governments as regards inwards investment, have also shaped the manner in which global corporations interact with governments and domestic corporations in locations where they seek to invest, not least through reactions to international arbitration (and the case law that has emerged from such cases).[4] One might also cite various global climate or natural environment focused treaties and conventions, that when refracted through domestic (or in the case of the European Union, regional) legislation have had considerable impact on how corporations may act and/or develop new investment(s) in plant and manufacturing processes.

As we move away from these more law-like aspects of global governance, there are other elements that while not strictly enforceable in their strictures, remain influential on corporations' activities and practices. These range from the work of the International Accounting Standards Board to standardize financial reporting—which is also reinforced by major national stock-markets requiring certain accounting standards to be fulfilled for listing, and thereby easier corporate access to financial resources—to trade associations which oversee standardized reporting or inspections regimes (such as those around aircraft safety). Here there are developed and applicable rules which, while lacking formal legal sanctions, remain relatively robust: for most corporations there are clear incentives for following the regulations, be it the ability to access investors in specific countries or to enter specific markets for services. At the weaker end of the spectrum are the guidelines to corporate behavior and practice put together by various organizations over the years, and which to an extent have culminated in the UN Global Compact. Appearing alongside these are the non-state surveillance and publicity-generating activities that contribute to "civil regulation";[5] here publicity, moral persuasion, and issues of legitimacy alongside brand management all play into non-state, social pressures on corporations to follow non-legal, but formalized rules, guidelines, and principles.

As this summary implies, it is very hard to establish in general the extent of the global corporate sector's exposure to global governance and the impact of such governance on its general shape or character. Rather, to understand the role of global governance there is a need to work on the basis of sectors and even individual corporations: certain corporations may be better placed than others to work with the regulations or guidelines, and indeed may use support for them as a way of raising barriers-to-entry for prospective competitors.[6] This can have a guild-like function when particular sectors establish global standards which (again) may work against new market entrants, or at the very least raise their costs of competing with the established corporations. For instance, many aspects of the regulatory structure of the European Union effectively raise the costs of market entry for corporations from outside the Union; internal to the EU, in the agriculture sector the Common Agricultural Policy has done much to facilitate the consolidation of the farm sector into ever larger agro-corporate concerns and away from the small farmers of the popular imagination. Of course, this is not to argue that these developments have been merely happenstance and the global corporate sector has had no role in influencing the development of global governance.

Global corporations' influence over global governance

As global corporations have been in some ways subject to global governance, it is no surprise that they have sought to influence and shape its form(s) and foci. This is hardly unjustified; historically legislation and regulation has developed through ongoing negotiation between the rulers and the ruled. Away from and before contemporary liberal democracy, such negotiation took various forms ranging from peaceful protest to violent insurrection, but in democracies at least there is a well-developed acceptance that societies or communities affected by the law and regulations have some rights to engage with legislators and regulators about the shape of such laws and rules. This may take place through formalized periodic voting, through political campaigns or via specialized lobbying. There is, however, an often commented on democratic deficit in global governance, but this does not make the interventions that global corporations can and have made over particular aspects of global governance necessarily un-democratic or illegitimate. Rather, especially since the emergence of an Internet-enfranchised global civil society, much of the discussion of the development of global governance as it relates to global corporations has become an increasingly well-developed public domain of discussion and argument. This is to say, while developing unevenly, what has now developed in the first decades of the new millennium is a political space where global corporations, states (and international organizations), and global civil society (and civil regulatory organizations) meet in a triangular debate about the regulation of, and social responsibilities of the corporate sector. Of course, the civil regulatory aspect of this triangle is in part a response to perceived failures in the state aspect of regulation,[7] but is also reflects a demand for non-state forms of regulatory legitimation (for instance around globalized sustainable sourcing practices).

In this new and still developing political domain, as I discussed in Chapter 4, corporations are able to deploy a range of power resources by which they seek to influence the development of global governance in their favor. In this they are no different to any other pressure or interest group, although it is also clear that large global corporations have significantly greater potential social political economic power than many other groups, because of the resources they control and their often privileged access to policy elites. However, this is not to say that therefore they are able to influence and shape the development of global governance unimpeded. Civil regulatory organizations, popular campaigns, and pressures put on democratic states have all led to some countervailing influence around the corporate political agenda. Nevertheless, this is dependent on the manner in which the issues reach the public realm; for instance, and discussed in the previous chapter, until recently the issue of global corporate taxation was seen as a technical issue in which only two aspects of the regulatory triangle outlined above had a legitimate interest. Political oversight of tax was seen in the corporate sector as interference, with a set of negotiations between a corporation and the civil service normally far from prying eyes of any democratic oversight. Again, though, in a time of ever expanding data and information availability, keeping such "negotiations" quiet and private is no longer as easy as it once was.

There is also little that is shared about the global corporate interest beyond the most general narrative elements discussed earlier around the depiction of the market, state-competitiveness, and the desirability of economic growth (delivered by the private sector). Indeed, it is not unusual to find different corporations on either side of a political debate (depending often on their size, history, and market interest) and, as such, for individual issues there is less likely to be a single corporate position, although for international issues there is more frequently a clustering of individual corporations differentiated by their globality (their exposure to, and integration with global markets).[8] Therefore, while corporate discursive power may be highly influential in setting the "mood music" of the global political economy, and this certainly benefits corporations, this benefit is hardly un-differentiated or uncontested. Moreover, increasingly, corporations' political power is dependent on their ability to maintain some semblance of public political legitimacy, an area where civil regulatory surveillance and activity can have its greatest impact.[9] Paradoxically, as Michael Moran has pointed out, just as "business becomes better at delivering the economic goods, and raises its standards of behavior, [it] is increasingly distrusted and despised."[10] Here the work of discursive power becomes not so much proactive and agenda-shaping, but defensive and about the maintenance of the favorable political agenda that was constructed when things seemed to be going better.

The largest global corporations may exhibit a centralization of control that suggests they are able to construct a coherent, self-interested, and influential political position as regards the global political economy, but as the 2008 financial crisis demonstrates in part, these large corporations are not indestructible or immune from material changes in the global system. Likewise, technological developments, geopolitical changes, or just incompetence can bring down corporations, and with the now heightened possibility of civil/social surveillance, the ability of corporations to act with impunity is fading if not entirely disappearing. Indeed, the very complexity of global supply chains and corporate networks, while sometimes making it difficult to appreciate where a regulatory intervention is most appropriate, also provides a wide range of interaction points at which regulatory or political pressure can be brought to bear on the global corporations' activity.[11] Thus, while corporations (rightly) are able to influence and negotiate around the regulatory regimes with which they interact, global civil society increasingly is able to balance such influence and at the very least ensure there is public discussion and knowledge about this realm of global governance; the vacuum caused by global governance's democratic deficit has been filled in various ways, and in the global corporate sector at least is becoming a vibrant space of contestation and growing civil engagement.

Global corporations as global governance institutions

I have also suggested at a number of points that by virtue of their organization, it may make sense to think of global corporations as institutions of global governance. Indeed, the expansion of guidelines, principles, and (internal) codes of conduct for global corporations itself might be read as the gradual establishment of a body of customary international law.[12] If these rules are asserted as applicable by corporations, then perhaps they should be able to be held to account through international legal action, albeit such action (as with all customary law) would be more about condemnation than major international political sanctioning. Whether a customary law case would lead to any stronger international normative reaction if it was brought to an international court (most likely the International Court of Justice) is as yet unknown, but does represent an interesting possibility. However, moving the argument in this direction does, as I have indicated, also suggest that it might make sense to consider global corporations as global governance institutions themselves. Global corporations are often engaged in the management of extremely complex networks of subsidiaries, affiliates, and contractors, and thus the realm over which they have influence (and power) is often global. Given that we already understand global governance as a diverse set of institutions across a fragmented and discontinuous political domain, it follows that we might also regard the management of a corporation's global complex as fulfilling a similar (partial, but global) governance function.

This governance function is underpinned by three aspects of the character of the corporation's supply and organizational network. Where the assets being deployed are not easily replicable outside the network, which is to say they are relatively specific to the network's needs (such as specialized technology, or particular skills in the workforce), the central controlling corporation has to develop an inspection function as the market does not offer alternatives that can be deployed to discipline constituent parts of the supply chain (the corporation cannot easily dismiss and renew network elements). Secondly, if demands in the end market require specific qualities, or processes to be adhered to for market advantage or to fulfill product regulations, again the network may be more closely governed, to ensure these conditions are fulfilled. Finally, regulations put in place by the corporation's home state may also be carried through to the entire network (for ease) by corporate management teams, although these considerations often play a somewhat lesser role.[13] All three elements prompt the development by corporations of governance function(s) across their networks, complete with administrative processes and evaluative mechanisms, that at the very least is analogous with, and in many ways directly parallels the more often recognized institutions of global governance.

Following David Ciepley, we can posit that "within its jurisdiction, the business corporation exercises powers analogous to those of government, if more limited including the right to command, regulate, adjudicate, set rules of cooperation, allocate collective resources, educate, discipline and punish."[14] However, while Ciepley is right that when compared with the sovereign state there is considerable difference in the scope and range of such legitimate capabilities, when we compare the global corporation with the typical institution of global governance these differences are considerably less significant, with the corporation often in a stronger position as regards its network than is an institution of global governance as related to its issue area (or constituent state members); corporations may well be able to more effectively sanction network members than some international organizations can.[15] Thus, the corporation can be understood within its own network as a form of governing body, adopting as Ciepley suggests many of the attributes of government; the authority it is able to mobilize, however, is not separate from government, but rather flows from the legal mechanisms (such as incorporation) that facilitate the corporation's operational modes.[16] This is to say, the corporation's governance function is not *against* the state, but rather is facilitated *by* the state.

Focusing on the global realm, these state facilitated attributes therefore indicate that corporations may have joined the ranks of institutions of global governance. Carrying their governance capabilities into the global arena, and focusing on their complex networks, the legitimated governance function they enjoy within the domestic economy can now be utilized across their networks and supply chains, and parallels the similar manner of constructing legitimacy that international governmental organizations rely on; the pull through from state sovereignty. Therefore, while global corporations certainly interact with the other institutions of global governance as discussed across the chapters of this volume, equally they also govern significant realms of the global political economy, sometimes in conjunction with the regulations and guidelines of other institutions, sometimes as single governing authorities themselves. It is this latter dimension that hitherto has been under-recognized in discussions and analyses of global governance.

Conclusion

The global corporation is with us and we should not expect that it will disappear, although its form(s) may shift and change again, or that all global corporations are necessarily particularly similar. Moreover, the plight of particular corporations is far from certain, rather the sector is relatively volatile with any particular decade's dominant corporations likely to find themselves successfully challenged in the future with newly growing corporations replacing them in (even the most oligopolistic) markets, as has been happening from the last century. For critics of the corporate sector this is of less importance than the collective structural power enjoyed by the (albeit fluid) corporate elite. I do not want to deny that Doris Fuchs' and Stephen Wilks' analysis of the discursive power has some credible purchase on the political economy of global corporations, but in the realm of global governance, as I am sure they would agree, this has to be tempered by the recognition of a range of countervailing social forces that cannot and should not be ignored.

In standard economic treatments of the market, the key counter-vailing force to the corporation is the consumer as sovereign market participant. Here, the legitimacy and acceptability of corporate behavior is tested each day in the market, although this relies on two key issues: firstly, the consumer has to have a good and trusted source of information about corporate practices and behavior so as to make reasoned and informed choices as regards those corporations that both fulfill the consumers' immediate economic needs and most nearly accord with their moral, ethical, political, or other preferences; secondly, enough consumers need to make their choices on this basis to favor particular corporations and by doing so boost their market share and profit. These successful corporations then spawn imitators who mimic their ethical stance and slowly the market facilitates a convergence on the preferences and values of a market society. To some extent the role of global governance would then merely be to ensure that information is reliable and available while also regulating other formal aspects of international economic relations. Indeed, consumer choice and the protection of a corporation's brand are sometimes cited as reasons why corporations are willing to engage with various civil regulatory initiatives but there is scant evidence that there is sufficient consumer interest to impact on *actual* financial performance or brand integrity, despite seemingly even corporations (at least half) believing it does.[17] However, equally the people who work for global corporations are like you and me: some may be mildly sociopathic and not care about their employers' reputation, but in the main it is quite likely that civil regulatory interventions are successful in part because those who work for their targeted corporations still want to feel good about their actions and work. All collective actors in the end are related to the actions of their constituent individuals and while corporations may not be natural persons, certainly they are run by natural persons.

Finally, one way of reading this book is that I have attempted to denaturalize corporations, revealing them to be (global) political economic institutions in themselves as well as key agents in the politics of global governance; this denaturalization is intended to demonstrate that (global) corporations are socially and legally constructed actors, and not at all the same as the natural persons on whom they have in some senses been (legally) modeled. As José Alvarez succinctly puts it: "We should never confuse the economic rights of corporations (or of investors) for the rights of natural persons to live in dignity."[18] We may recognize that corporations have legitimate rights, but in the end to conflate those rights with human rights is to make a category error and by doing so elevate corporations' rights beyond their legitimate and acceptable level. Thus, when we consider the place of corporations in global governance, we should not be making any direct use of the metaphor (explicit or implicit) between corporate rights and human rights. It may make things easier to consider if we just see these as two forms of rights under global governance, but in the end corporations are not people and thus need to be treated in a way appropriate to their political economy and their socio-political place in global society. Only then can we establish an account of global corporations and global governance that is neither too accommodating to special interests, nor too hysterical in its suspicion of legitimate globalized economic activity and organization. If you have got to this point and now feel you can only understand the relationship between global corporations and global governance by examining some specific cases, then my work here is done.

Notes

1 Frederick Pohl and Cyril Kornbluth, *The Space Merchants* (New York: Galaxy Publishing Corp., 1953 [reprinted: London: Victor Gollancz, 1972]).
2 Now that the International Criminal Court is able to detain war criminals one cannot say that no natural persons are subject to international law!
3 Christopher May, "The Corruption of the Public Interest: Intellectual Property and the Corporation as a Rights Holding 'Citizen'" in *The Challenges of Global Business Authority: Democratic Renewal, Stalemate, or Decay*, ed. T. Porter and K. Ronit (Albany: State University of New York Press, 2010): 179–201.
4 There is a large literature on international arbitration which we have not touched on, see for instance: Yves Dezalay and Bryant G. Garth, *Dealing in Virtue: International Commercial Arbitration and the Construction of a Transnational Legal Order* (Chicago. Ill.: Chicago University Press 1996); or Gus van Harten, *Investment Treaty Arbitration and Public Law* (Oxford: Oxford University Press, 2007).
5 David Vogel, "The Private Regulation of Global Corporate Conduct: Achievements and Limitations," *Business and Society* 49, no. 1 (2010): 68–87.
6 See: Cornelia Woll, *Firm Interests: How Governments Shape Business Lobbying on Global Trade* (Ithaca, NY: Cornell University Press, 2008), for a nuanced discussion of how the variances and shifts in direction have played out in the governance of trade, telecommunications services, and international air transport; here the role of the EU as a modifier and shaper of corporate positions and strategies is of special interest.
7 Vogel, "The Private Regulation of Global Corporate Conduct," 73.
8 At the time of writing (Summer 2014), before the referendum on Scottish Independence, both yes and no campaigns have vocal and well organized groups of businesses supporting their side.
9 Doris Fuchs, *Business Power in Global Governance* (Boulder, Colo.: Lynne Rienner Publishers, 2007), 167.

10 Michael Moran, *Business, Politics and Society: An Anglo-American Comparison* (Oxford: Oxford University Press, 2009), 167.
11 John Gerard Ruggie, *Just Business: Multinational Corporations and Human Rights* (New York: W.W. Norton & Co., 2013), xxxiv.
12 Gregory T. Euteneier, "Towards a Corporate 'Law of Nations': Multinational Enterprises' contributions to Customary International Law," *Tulane Law Review* 82 (December 2007): 758–780.
13 Adrienne Héritier, Anna Kristen Müller-Debus, and Christian R. Thauer, "The Responsible Corporation: Regulating the Supply Chain" in *The Responsible Corporation in a Global Economy*, ed. C. Crouch and C. Maclean (Oxford: Oxford University Press, 2011), 119–140.
14 David Ciepley, "Beyond Public and Private: Toward a Political Theory of the Corporation," *American Political Science Review* 107, no. 1 (February 2013): 142.
15 See also Pierre-Yves Néron, "Business and the Polis: What Does it Mean to See Corporations as Political Actors," *Journal of Business Ethics* 94 (2010): 344–349, on the difficulty in the national political realm of making a direct link between the corporation and the state as agents of governance; however, many of Néron's qualifications (the differences in ability to "exit" the state and the corporation, the latter of which one can merely resign from or end a contract; the focus on aims and purposes is differently decided and legitimated; members of states—citizens—are formally equal in a way the hierarchy of the corporation does not really recognize) fall away when corporations are compared with institutions of global governance, as such institutions are in these dimensions more like corporations than states.
16 Ciepley, "Beyond Public and Private," 151.
17 Vogel, "The Private Regulation of Global Corporate Conduct," 77.
18 José E. Alvarez, "Are Corporations 'Subjects' of International Law," *Santa Clara Journal of International Law* 9, no. 1 (2011): 35; and see Robert R. Reich, *Supercapitalism: The Transformation of Business, Democracy and Everyday Life* (New York: Alfred A Knopf, 2007), Chapter 6, for an extended set of arguments for why it is anti-democratic for corporations to be treated in a similar manner to natural persons *qua* citizens.

Select Bibliography

The following books and articles have been particularly useful in assembling the account presented in this book, and while they do not necessarily directly parallel my own argument(s), all are worth reading in preparation for any work on global corporations and global governance.

Joel Bakan, *The Corporation: The Pathological Pursuit of Profit and Power* (New York: Free Press, 2004).
Bakan's analysis places a considerable weight on the legal establishment of legal personality and asks: what if we took the metaphor of the corporate person to its logical end by offering a psychoanalytical account of the corporation? Along the way Bakan develops a number of interesting insights into how the corporate legal form influences managerial behavior(s) and decisions.

John Braithwaite and Peter Drahos, *Global Business Regulation* (Cambridge: Cambridge University Press, 2000).
This book is a vital reference source for anyone looking at the global governance of the corporate sector, offering both analytical models and a wide range of sector-by-sector accounts of the myriad spaces of regulation. Each sector is treated historically before a political economic analysis relating the general approach to the particular is presented and represents a still vital resource some 15 years after appearing.

William K. Carroll and Jean Phillipe Sapinski, "The Global Corporate Elite and the Transnational Policy-Planning Network 1996–2006: A Structural Analysis," *International Sociology* 25, no. 4 (2010): 501–538.
This interesting piece of data analysis develops a map and account of the interactions between the global corporate managerial and the global policy making elites. While in one sense confirming many suspicions critics have harbored for years, this is refreshingly data driven with a nuanced and complex picture of the network of interactions that (at least partly) inform the global governance of the corporate sector.

David Ciepley, "Beyond Public and Private: Toward a Political Theory of the Corporation," *American Political Science Review* 107, no. 1 (February 2013): 139–158.
Ciepley's work, while focused on the USA has considerable salience for a general account of the political role and place of the corporation in society. This and other work he has developed argues strongly against the separation of corporate affairs and (global) politics.

Hugh Compston, "The network of global corporate control: implications for public policy," *Business and Politics* 15, no. 3 (2013): 357–379.
Complementing Carroll and Sapinski's work, this article looks at the intra-sectoral networks of control patterning the global corporate realm, examining how cross shareholdings and corporate ownership have centralized the effective control of corporate affairs in a relatively focused group of (often financial sector) corporations. Again, based on extensive data analysis, this sometimes confirms the suspicions of corporate critics, but also presents a richly detailed picture of global corporate ownership and control.

John H. Dunning and Sarianna Lundan, *Multinational Enterprises and the Global Economy* (second edition) (Cheltenham: Edward Elgar, 2008).
In this book Dunning and Lundan assemble a multifaceted and extensive account of the global corporation across a wide range of topics. This is an excellent starting place for readers unfamiliar with the complexities of global corporations' practices and structures.

Kevin Farnsworth, *Social Versus Corporate Welfare: Competing Needs and Interests within the Welfare State* (Basingstoke: Palgrave Macmillan, 2012).
Farnsworth's insightful book examines the manner in which corporations benefit from states' provision of services and social stability. This is a useful corrective to the idea that the corporate sector benefits from or is interested in reducing the role of the state in the economy to a minimum.

Doris Fuchs, *Business Power in Global Governance* (Boulder, Colo.: Lynne Rienner Publishers, 2007).
In this book Fuchs develops a number of themes about the power of global corporations in global governance. She is especially concerned with the manner in which influence over the narrative of the global market allows corporations to structure global governance to their own advantage.

Michael Moran, *Business, Politics and Society: An Anglo-American Comparison* (Oxford: Oxford University Press, 2009).
Moran has written a well-developed account of the role that corporations play in national political economies, based explicitly on the history of this interaction in the UK and the USA. The book does, however, offer a number of insights about corporate practices and policy processes which are likely to

have a wider application than merely the states' histories from which they are derived.

Mark J. Roe, *Political Determinants of Corporate Governance: Political Context, Corporate Impact* (Oxford: Oxford University Press, 2003).
Focusing on corporate governance this more technical book develops a useful analysis of how political structures have an impact on corporate governance. Roe uses a rather broad political brush, but nonetheless the analysis offers some useful tools that can be applied in more focused analysis.

John Gerard Ruggie, *Just Business: Multinational Corporations and Human Rights* (New York: W.W. Norton & Co., 2013).
Ruggie was one of the key players in the establishment of the UN Global Compact, and before that had a long and distinguished academic career as a political economist. This book offers reflections on his attempt to take this analytical position and use it to inform an intervention in the governance of the global corporate political economy; as such, it is a very interesting read for anyone thinking about the impact of their research in this (or any other) issue area.

David Vogel, "The Private Regulation of Global Corporate Conduct: Achievements and Limitations," *Business and Society* 49, no. 1 (2010): 68–87.
This article is a key source for thinking about the manner in which global civil society has developed its countervailing power in the global corporate sector. Vogel's account sets out what can and has been achieved, and also what constrains the ability of global civil society to fully shape corporate activity.

Michael C. Webb, "Shaping International Corporate Taxation," in *Global Corporate Power* (IPE Yearbook 15), ed. C. May (Boulder, Colo.: Lynne Rienner Publishers, 2006).
This chapter, from my edited collection on *Global Corporate Power* offers one of the best and concise accounts of the problems with developing a fully globalized system of corporate taxation. Webb's work (as readers will appreciate) greatly influenced the account I offer in Chapter 5 of this book and as such is directly complementary to the analysis offered there.

Stephen Wilks, *The Political Power of the Business Corporation* (Cheltenham: Edward Elgar, 2013).
Like the Moran book, Wilks takes a mainly national view, but develops a number of key arguments about the character and processes of corporate political influence. Again there is much here that is directly applicable beyond the empirical focus in which it has been developed.

Index

Routledge Global Institutions Series

The International Monetary Fund (2nd edition)
Politics of conditional lending
by James Raymond Vreeland (Georgetown University)

The UN Global Compact
by Catia Gregoratti (Lund University)

Institutions for Women's Rights
by Charlotte Patton (York College, CUNY) and
Carolyn Stephenson (University of Hawaii)

International Aid
by Paul Mosley (University of Sheffield)

Global Consumer Policy
by Karsten Ronit (University of Copenhagen)

The Changing Political Map of Global Governance
by Anthony Payne (University of Sheffield) and
Stephen Robert Buzdugan (Manchester Metropolitan University)

Coping with Nuclear Weapons
by W. Pal Sidhu

Global Governance and China
The dragon's learning curve
edited by Scott Kennedy (Indiana University)

The Politics of Global Economic Surveillance
by Martin S. Edwards (Seton Hall University)

Mercy and Mercenaries
Humanitarian agencies and private security companies
by Peter Hoffman

Regional Organizations in the Middle East
by James Worrall (University of Leeds)

Reforming the UN Development System
The Politics of Incrementalism
by Silke Weinlich (Duisburg-Essen University)

The United Nations as a Knowledge Organization
by Nanette Svenson (Tulane University)

The International Criminal Court
The Politics and practice of prosecuting atrocity crimes
by Martin Mennecke (University of Copenhagen)

The Politics of International Organizations
Views from insiders
edited by Patrick Weller (Griffith University) and
Xu Yi-chong (Griffith University)

The African Union (2nd edition)
Challenges of globalization, security, and governance
by Samuel M. Makinda (Murdoch University),
F. Wafula Okumu (African Union), and
David Mickler (University of Western Australia)

BRICS
by João Pontes Nogueira (Catholic University, Rio de Janeiro) and
Monica Herz (Catholic University, Rio de Janeiro)

Expert Knowledge in Global Trade
edited by Erin Hannah (University of Western Ontario),
James Scott (University of Manchester), and
Silke Trommer (Murdoch University)

The European Union (2nd edition)
Clive Archer (Manchester Metropolitan University)

Governing Climate Change (2nd edition)
Peter Newell (University of East Anglia) and
Harriet A. Bulkeley (Durham University)

Contemporary Human Rights Ideas (2nd edition)
Betrand Ramcharan (Geneva Graduate Institute of
International and Development Studies)

Protecting the Internally Displaced
Rhetoric and reality
Phil Orchard (University of Queensland)

The Arctic Council
Within the far north
Douglas C. Nord (Umea University)

For further information regarding the series, please contact:

Nicola Parkin, Editor, Politics & International Studies
Taylor & Francis
2 Park Square, Milton Park, Abingdon
Oxford OX14 4RN, UK
Nicola.parkin@tandf.co.uk
www.routledge.com